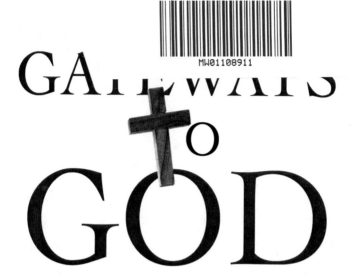

GATEWAYS TO GOD

GATEWAYS

✝o

GOD

Remove Your Roadblocks
and Live His Love

by DMITRI BILGERE

Reveal Mercy Press
MADISON, WI

GATEWAYS TO GOD:
Remove Your Roadblocks and Live His Love

Design and production: Kristyn Kalnes
Author photo: Sans Talbot

Published in the United States by Reveal Mercy Press

ISBN 978-0-9891037-1-8

Contents

Get out of God's Way and into God's Love

"You're one of the best things to ever happen to me," the woman I intended to marry told me. "And I can never talk to you again."

I was almost forty years old, and every woman I'd ever wanted to marry had broken up with me, abruptly and out of the blue. Bizarrely, these women had often used exactly the same words: "You're one of the best things to ever happen to me. And I can never talk to you again."

This pattern was especially upsetting because, at this point in my career, I'd spent almost fifteen years helping **other people** create the lives they wanted. I'd run workshops all over North America, Europe, and South Africa. I'd trained leaders. I'd written a relationship book that was used in university classrooms. I'd helped clients—truly helped them—get through every kind of upsetting life experience you can imagine. I'd even helped single people get married.

But for all that, I couldn't help myself. Every few years I'd meet another "woman of my dreams." We'd be crazy about each other and then—abruptly, bafflingly—she'd leave.

But today, as this current woman was telling me that oh-so-familiar story of how great I'd been for her and how she could never talk to me again, something different happened. Time appeared to slow down. Her voice seemed to slur to a halt. Between her words, a space opened.

And in that space, a thought appeared in my mind. It was crystal clear and absolutely certain:

"No matter what I do, I can't fix this."

That idea was new to me. In spite of my many relationship failures, I'd never given up on the idea that I could eventually fix this problem and marry the woman of my dreams. I had never before considered that the problem might, in fact, be something I could never fix.

And then the thought repeated just as clearly, but this time with an emphasis on the word "I."

"No matter what **I** do, **I** can't fix this."

And let me tell you, I had tried. I had made lists of what my perfect woman would be like, of my "must haves" and my "deal breakers." I had hired the best counselors I could find—arguably some of the best in the world—to help me clear away any psychological blocks I might have had against getting married. I had done whatever it took to make myself attractive to the kind of woman I desired.

I had done everything a man could do, and none of it had worked.

No matter what **I** did, **I** couldn't fix this.

Then, into that same clear space, came this thought:

"If I were God, and I wanted to show Dmitri that he is **not** God—which, quite frankly, he sometimes gets confused about—I would give him the relationship of his dreams and then snatch it away from him, over and over, until he was finally driven to his knees before Me."

That thought was so surprising that I probably seemed distracted to my soon-to-be-former girlfriend. What if God had set up these relationship failures as a way of bringing me closer to **Him**?

And what if every action I had taken to "solve the problem" of my being single had actually pushed me in the wrong direction, ever more focused on my own actions, and had gotten in the way of what God wanted to give me?

I sat stunned by my new insight as the now-former love of my life finished breaking up with me and left. But the truth was, I hardly heard her. I was too astounded by the idea that everything I'd being doing to "fix" my relationship problem might actually be getting in the way of what God wanted to give me.

And the following Sunday, I started going to church.

Now, this story has a happy ending. Several years later I met the woman who became my wife. And that relationship is so amazing, so surprising, and so intimate that I'm grateful none of those other relationships worked out. I'd say my wife is the woman of my dreams, but my dreams were never this good.

But my marriage would never have happened if I hadn't had that moment of clarity, when I saw that the actions I was taking were actually getting in the way of what God wanted to give me.

The Five Christian Roadblocks

I tell you this story because, in my years of working with Christians, both as a one-on-one phone coach and as a workshop leader, I've seen that a similar dynamic often happens to them.

Just as I wanted a closer relationship with a woman, Christians want a closer relationship with God. But **just as the actions I took to get closer to a woman actually got in the way of what God wanted to give me, too often the actions Christians take to get closer to God get in the way of the love and the mercy that God wants to give them.**

As you'll discover in this book, there are five distinct actions that Christians take in the hopes of getting closer to God that actually get in the way. They are the five Christian Roadblocks:

> Christians try to get closer to God by ignoring their lives.
>
> Christians try to get closer to God by "balancing the books" with God.
>
> Christians try to get closer to God by making Christianity into a checklist.
>
> Christians try to get closer to God by suffering through repentance.
>
> Christians try to get closer to God by having a "mercy exception."

Just as the actions I took to get myself closer to marriage actually got in the way of what God wanted to give me, these "Christian Roadblocks" are actions we take that get in the way of our experiencing closeness with God.

The Purpose of this Book

My purpose in writing this book is simple: I wrote about the gateways to God with the prayer in my heart that they would be a revelation of God's love and God's mercy for you. Not "love and mercy" as an idea, but "love and mercy" as a continuous, moment-by-moment way of living that inspires you, guides you, loves you, and comforts you.

We owe our awareness of the Gateways to God to the teachings, life, sacrifice and resurrection of Jesus Christ. Christ **is** the gateway; he came so that we might reclaim our birthright of closeness with God. Through his life he modeled and taught this closeness, and through his sacrifice we are granted the mercy and the love from which we are commanded to live.

Because Jesus Christ is the gateway to God, I've written each of the five gateways in this book to reveal an aspect of Christ's love, and how we can incorporate it—deeply, daily—into our lives.

It's my intention that these gateways help you feel God's love and mercy for you in all aspects of your life: no matter who you are, no matter what you've done, no matter how you feel, and no matter what your life circumstances are.

How This Book Is Organized

To that end I have kept this book as simple as possible: the book is short, and each of the five main chapters has a similar structure. Each chapter will walk you through a Christian Mercy, a Christian Roadblock, a Christian Challenge and, finally, a Christian Gateway.

Let me explain each of these:

THE CORE CHRISTIAN MERCIES. When I became Christian, I was surprised to discover what I've since come to think of as the "Core Mercies of Christianity." I was surprised because, profound as these mercies are, I'd never heard most of them before I became a Christian. As Christians we take these mercies for granted, but they are, in fact, some of our greatest blessings. And even though Christians know about these mercies, we often don't experience the true impact of them. In each chapter we'll explore one of these mercies and the impact it can have on your life.

THE CHRISTIAN ROADBLOCKS. Christians are on a journey to closeness with God, and the Christian Roadblocks are the actions we take in pursuit of that closeness that actually get in the way of our achieving it. Each chapter discusses a roadblock and includes an example of that roadblock in someone's life, to help you identify it when it gets in the way of your closeness with your Lord.

THE CHRISTIAN CHALLENGES. Living in the experience of God's love and God's mercy goes against our fallen human nature, so living that experience is challenging. In each chapter I'll share the Christian challenge that accompanies that chapter's core mercy, so you won't be surprised by that challenge when it confronts you in your life.

THE GATEWAYS TO GOD. For each challenge, there is a gateway that opens you to the experience of God's love. In my experience, these five gateways represent the "five essential moves" of Christianity. They are where "the rubber meets the road" in our experience of closeness with God. Each chapter will show you how to walk through a gateway, and each chapter will equip you with a tool you can use right away to experience a deeper closeness with God.

Along the way, I'll shares stories, examples, and metaphors to make everything simple, clear, and easy to use in your life.

Online Extras

To keep this book short, while still offering more information to readers who want to explore topics in greater depth, I've included "online extras." In some chapters you'll see a section like this one. It contains a link to an "online extra"—more writing or a video that expands on a topic, answers more questions about a topic, or addresses unusual circumstances that sometimes arise when people try to apply these teachings to their lives. You don't need to access the online extras to get the benefits of this book, but if you are interested in exploring a topic more deeply, the online extras are available for you.

And if you are truly interested in experiencing and living from God's love and mercy in your daily life, you will probably want to know about my website and blog, at GatewaysToGod.com. At the website I regularly answer questions and share tips and tools to help you feel God's love and God's mercy in every area of your life, every day. You can also follow me on twitter @DmitriBilgere, and connect with me by "liking" me on Facebook at Facebook.com/DmitriBilgere.

HERE'S THE FIRST ONLINE EXTRA: A video greeting from me to you, the reader of this book. Even though we probably haven't met in person, I admire you for investigating these ideas and for pursuing a life of living in God's love and God's mercy. My brief online "hello" is a way to start our relationship with one another. It's at

GatewaysToGod.com/hello

> >

And of course you can always contact me at db@GatewaysToGod.com, or by using the contact form you'll find at GatewaysToGod.com. I strive to answer every question sent to me, so ask me anything as we get to know one another.

What You'll Get From this Book

This book is not a book of theory: I've designed it to be as immediately useful as possible. Here are the three core benefits you can expect to get from understanding the Christian Roadblocks and Gateways to God:

CORE BENEFIT NUMBER 1: You'll get better at the "nuts and bolts" of experiencing God's love and God's mercy for you. One of the great benefits of Christianity is that it offers a life in which God's love and mercy is available to you—for real, no fooling, every moment of every day.

But just because God's love and mercy is always available to you does not necessarily mean you are good at experiencing it. In fact, if my years of working with Christians have taught me one thing, it's that many of us **don't** know how to experience the love and the mercy God has for us.

Therefore, the big question is **not** "Does God have love and mercy for you?" You know the answer to that one: He does—so much, in fact, that He sent His Son to redeem you. The big question is, are you experiencing that love and that mercy, in your heart, every day?

This book will help you rediscover and more deeply experience the truth of God's love and God's mercy for you, as a real, living, breathing, flowing experience.

CORE BENEFIT NUMBER 2: You'll get better at returning to the experience of God's love and mercy when you have strayed from it. As important as it is to be able to experience God's love and God's mercy, that alone is not enough to guarantee you a full Christian life. That's because our human nature is to stray from our closeness with God. You need the skills to be able to get back to the experience of His love when you have strayed. Otherwise, the experience of straying away from God can easily turn into the experience of **staying away** from God.

You might think that Christians would automatically return to the experience of God's love, but many of us do not. A client of mine once described the problem perfectly. She said, "When I'm in touch with God's love for me, I can't imagine ever wanting to leave it. But when I'm **not** in touch with His love for me, I can't even remember that it exists! When I'm turned away, I feel as if being 'on my own' is my natural state.

I don't even think to try to turn back to Him. It's as if that love doesn't even exist."

When you understand the Christian roadblocks, you'll be better able to notice when you have turned away from God's love. You'll be able to diagnose where you've "gone off track" in your closeness with God, and to re-open the gateways to the experience of His love.

CORE BENEFIT NUMBER 3: **You'll get better at living your life, with all its challenges, guided and energized by God's love and God's mercy.** A workshop participant once told me, "I'm really great at feeling God's love when I'm alone in a beautiful place. I can even return to God's love when conditions are right. But when I go back to the 'real world,' I lose that sense of love. Suddenly I'm stressed out, I'm losing my temper, and it's like that experience of His love never even happened."

Christ tells us to love God…and then immediately tells us also to love our neighbors as we love ourselves. I often wonder if part of the reason he told us to love our neighbors might be that our relationships with other people—and, by extension, with the world at large—are the laboratory for practicing our expression of our love of God, and for practicing receiving His love for us.

I suspect that many of us, however, aren't so good at "loving our neighbors." We are more like that workshop participant: We find it easier to act from God's love when we are alone in a peaceful place than when we are confronted by the "real world." We become like Linus in an early "Peanuts" comic strip, saying, "I love humanity. It's **people** I can't stand!"

It's important that you know the "nuts and bolts" of how to experience the reality of God's love and mercy for you (core benefit number 1). It's also important that you know how to return to the experience of His love when you've strayed from it (core benefit number 2).

But it does you little good to have the experience of God's love and God's mercy for you, and even to be able to return to it, if you aren't also able to **take action in your life from that love and that mercy,** moment by moment, day by day.

This book is not about feeling God's love in a vacuum; it's about building His kingdom in the world through how you behave, day in and day out. To that end, I'll share specific tools that will not only help you feel and return to His love and His mercy, but will also help you be empowered and guided by that love and mercy as you live your day-to-day life.

Living a Graceful and Gracious Life

Authentically experiencing God's love and God's mercy, returning to it when you have strayed, and acting from it as you face the daily challenges of your life: These are, I believe, the elements of living a graceful and gracious Christian life.

And even though it might seem like that is asking a lot of life, I believe that such a life is what Christ wants for us. As he tells us in John 10:10 (a verse to which we will return many times in this book), "I came that they may have life, and have it abundantly."

Your life will probably not always go the way you would prefer. God may not always give you what you want when you want it. But His love and His mercy are always available to transform you, in any situation, into what He desires for you to be.

Our journey begins with a man I'll call Gary, at the beginning of a weekend I was running for Christian men...

Gateway One: Seek

"I just want to be closer to God," Gary said.

I looked at the slim, handsome, mid-forties man who was standing in front of me. He was obviously sincere. He did want to be closer to God.

And he'd been trying to get closer. He'd been trying hard.

It was the first day of a weekend seminar I was running for Christian men. Sometimes I ask participants, "What do you want, for yourself, from this weekend?" I had just asked Gary that question.

I waited for him to elaborate, and noticed he was actually starting to sweat.

I knew that Gary knew he'd given me the "right" answer. After all, what Christian wouldn't want to be closer to God? Who would claim that "I want to be closer to God" was the wrong answer?

But I also knew that Christians sometimes answer "I want to be closer to God" when they want to say something true, but not share anything personal about their lives. To dig a little deeper, I asked him, "If you got closer to God, what parts of your life would be better?"

Gary paused and thought about it. "Well," he said at last, "my relationship with my wife would be better, I guess."

"Tell me more about that. How is that relationship going?"

A look of authentic grief passed over Gary's face. "It's hardly going at all. She left me a few weeks ago, and took the kids with her. She says she's filing for divorce."

"Wow," I said. "That sounds upsetting."

"Yes." He shrugged. "But you know, the Lord moves in mysterious ways."

"That is absolutely true," I said. "But tell me: how do you handle your relationships with your wife and kids when those relationships become troubled?"

"I just try to ignore my earthly problems and turn to God more. I try to spend more time in the Word. I feel like if I could just get closer to Him, He'd take care of it."

"And how is that working?"

Gary's voice broke, revealing some of the frustration and sadness that I'd sensed were there: "I keep trying to get closer to Him, but things in my life just keep getting worse!"

Core Christian Mercy Number One

The first core Christian mercy I want to remind you of is the mercy that

> God's love is with you in every
> moment of your life.

It's true: "Neither life nor death, neither angels nor demons, neither height nor depth, nor anything else in creation will be able to separate us from the love of God" (Romans 8:38-39).

God's love is equally available everywhere in your life, no matter what. In good times and bad, in abasement and abounding, His love is always available to you. Nothing in creation—neither angels nor demons—can separate you from His love.

God's love, then, is **not** like your mobile phone's service: good in some areas, and spotty or completely absent in others. His love for you is everywhere in your life, at all times, equally.

Christian Roadblock Number One

But, as I said in the last chapter, just because His love is always available for you does **not** mean you are good at experiencing it. As we'll see, one of the surest ways to interfere with your experience of God's love is to ignore what's going on in your life.

That's Christian Roadblock Number One:

> Christians try to get closer to
> God by ignoring their lives.

Trying to get closer to God by ignoring your life is a problem because when Christians **ignore** their lives, they miss out on seeing how God is with them **in** their lives.

It was as if Gary was saying, "I have problems. I should ignore those problems, and the feelings I have about them, and focus on getting closer to God. If I can only get closer to God, those problems will automatically go away."

But that's the opposite of what really works. If God is with you in your life, you have to be in your life in order to experience how God is with you in it. That's the opposite of what many Christians do. It's the opposite of what Gary was doing.

You may have heard the country music song that advises that "if you are going through hell, keep going." To "keep going" means to participate in your life: to face and properly handle all the emotions you experience when it seems like you are going through hell. To keep going does **not** mean ignoring your emotions or experiences, or pretending that they aren't happening at all.

When we Christians experience upsetting circumstances in our lives, we sometimes try to get away from those experiences by telling ourselves to "give it to God," or to "lean on God," or to "let go and let God." We also sometimes tell ourselves that "with God all things are possible," or "you're never given more than you can handle," or that "the Lord moves in mysterious ways."

Those are important truths. It's a good idea to give your life to God, and to lean on God, and so on. It's also true that "with God all things are possible" (Matthew 19:26). And you don't have to be alive for very long to realize that the Lord moves in mysterious ways.

But if you use those truths as excuses to avoid dealing with the upsetting experiences and emotions of your life, you'll just be trying to "pray it away." You won't get to see how God is with you in your life because you won't be participating. When you avoid your life you aren't **in** your life, so you can't experience how **God is in your life with you**.

I asked Gary, "How is it working for you to turn away from your life to get closer to God? Is it giving you happiness? Is it giving you peace?"

He looked at me sadly. "I wish I could say it was, but I'm brokenhearted about how my life is going. I'm brokenhearted about my wife leaving me, and about my family. I try to ignore all that and go to God, but I just keep feeling more and more alone."

Remember, nothing in creation can separate us from the love of God, so God's love was still with Gary, even in during his difficult times. But Gary couldn't experience that love, because he himself wasn't present with the difficulty. He wasn't participating in his life. He was ignoring it "to get closer to God."

And that wasn't working.

Christian Challenge Number One

If "ignoring your life to get closer to God" is the first Christian roadblock, the first challenge of Christianity is:

To participate in your life, with
all its messiness, as your path for
getting closer to God.

My friend James Keeley likes to say, "God went to a lot of effort to set up the circumstances of your life, exactly the way they are, to guide you into becoming what God wants you to become." The idea is that you don't know what God means to make of you. Therefore you don't know the experiences you need to have in order to become the person He wants you to become.

That's the way of thinking you need to adopt if you are going to accept the Christian Challenge of participating in your life. The messiness of your life isn't some problem you have to get rid of. It's actually the path to take you where God wants you to go. But you won't experience transformation on that path if you won't participate in your life, with all its messiness, and discover how God's love is with you in it.

Online Extra: Blocks into Stepping Stones

In this Online Extra, I share my conversation with a friend that convinced me that what I think of as "blocks" in my life are actually stepping-stones on the path to closeness with God. Check it out at

GatewaysToGod.com/blocks

The Christian Challenge Is Hard

Sometimes we Christians seem to think that Christianity is a "free pass" that lets us avoid facing life's painful experiences. It's not. One of the blessings of our faith is that it is a way to **face** and **move through** your upsets, so that each difficulty draws you closer to God and transforms you even more into the person He is calling you to be. But it's hard: you have to face the feelings you have about what's happening in your life if you want to experience how God is close to you **in** your life.

And the way to start that process is summed up in one word: **Seek.**

Gateway to God Number One: Seek

If you want to be closer to God, you have to seek God. The Bible tells us this, not just once, but over and over. It's not an obscure bit of guidance, or some confusing, offhand directive. It's not like the "Bible quote" cartoon character Homer Simpson once made up, which he claimed would be found in the Bible, "somewhere near the back." We're told that we need to seek God, and we're told that often.

Here are just a few examples:

"Seek the Lord and His strength; seek His presence continually!" (1 Chronicles 16:11)

"Those who seek Me find Me." (Proverbs 8:17)

"I love those who love Me, and those who seek Me diligently find Me." (Proverbs 8:17)

"Seek the Lord, and His strength: seek His face evermore." (Psalm 105:4)

"Seek first the kingdom of God and His righteousness, and all these things will be added to you." (Matthew 6:33)

And if that isn't enough, we have it from our highest example: Christ himself. In Luke 5:16 we learn that "Jesus himself frequently withdrew to the wilderness and prayed." I was thunderstruck when I first read that: If Christ, the Son of God, took the time to seek the Father, it's probably a good idea for you and me to seek Him, too.

Seek God with All Your Heart and All Your Soul

So seeking God is a good idea. I agree. You agree. Gary agrees. Now the big question remains: how do you do it? Fortunately we are given some guidance for that, as well:

"…seek the Lord your God, and you will find Him if you search for Him with all your heart and all your soul." (Deuteronomy 4:29)

"You will seek Me and find Me when you seek Me with all your heart." (Jeremiah 29:13)

"Blessed are those who…seek Him with all their heart." (Psalm 119:2)

The Bible doesn't say, "Seek God through your smartest thoughts about God." It doesn't say, "Seek God with your best analysis of what your life ought to be like." And it doesn't say, "Seek God by running away from your feelings and from the problems of your life."

It says to seek Him with your heart and with your soul. (For the purposes of this book, I'm going to shorten "your heart and your soul" to simply "your heart," because I think in this context they go together.)

This is a big deal: You have to seek God with your heart. But if you are going to seek God with your heart, that means that you have to be in touch with your heart, and in touch with everything that is going on in your heart. After all, if you are trying to avoid your heart, how can you hope to seek God with it?

Acknowledging Your Feelings Puts You in Touch with Your Heart

When the Bible says neither life nor death, neither angels nor demons, neither height nor depth, nor anything else in creation will be able to separate you from the love of God, it isn't saying you should ignore those things.

If there are demons in your life, you need to face them. If there are angels in your life, you need to thank God for them. If you are lifted to a great height, or buried to a great depth, you need to acknowledge your feelings about those experiences.

Pretending there are no angels or demons in your life is the surest way to detach from what is going on in your heart. And if you aren't in touch with your heart, you won't be able to seek God with it.

Everyone's heart gets upset from time to time, because upsetting things happen in our lives. Your heart can get upset by something as big as a death, or as small as a busy workday. There are no rules for what can upset your heart.

Gary had an upset heart. His wife had left him. He was in danger of losing his children. When he ran away from that upset, he lost track of his heart. And **when Gary lost track of his heart, he lost his ability to seek God with his heart.**

Opening the Gateway of Seeking God

Being in touch with your heart opens the gateway to seeking God because when you get in touch with what's going on in your heart, you also get in touch with your neediness for God. And that neediness for God automatically starts you seeking Him.

I think the power of "neediness" in helping people seek may be what Jesus is talking about when he says "blessed are the poor in spirit: for theirs is the kingdom of heaven" (Matthew 5:3). Unless you actually experience your neediness for God—that is, unless you experience how you are poor in spirit, and how you need God because of it—you won't experience the kingdom of heaven, because you won't seek for it with "all your heart." If you don't experience your neediness, seeking the kingdom of heaven will just be an idea.

Consider the difference between saying "I need air to breathe" and trying to stay underwater for five minutes without taking a breath. The first is an idea about need: "Air is a good idea." The second is an experience of need: "I must have air right now!" If you're going to seek God with all your heart, you have to experience your need for God like a person trapped underwater experiences his or her need for air. It can't just be theoretical. It has to be urgent.

Feeling the need for God—not just theorizing about it—is the fuel that drives us in our seeking. And seeking God, as we are told so often, is the key to finding Him.

If Gary had been honest about what was going on in his heart, he would have been a puddle of need for God, and resolute in his intention to seek Him. He would have said, "God, I am hurting with what's going on in my life, I am needy for your help, and I am seeking You with all my heart." But because he was ignoring the feelings of his heart, he wasn't motivated to seek God like a person trapped underwater is motivated to seek air. His need was just a theory, an idea. He didn't know his need on a heart level, so he had little motivation to actually seek God.

Online Extra: God's Power Made Perfect in Weakness

It's sometimes said that the wisest person is the one who most knows his or her weakness before God. God told Paul, "My grace is sufficient for you, for My power is made perfect in weakness" (2 Corinthians 12:9). Discover more about how God's mercy flows toward need and weakness in this Online Extra, at

GatewaysToGod.com/weakness

Living the Christian Life of Seeking

It's easy to tell when you are motivated to seek God. You are motivated to seek God when you can truthfully speak this sentence:

"I am needy for You, O Lord, in my [whatever your circumstance is]."

You don't say "I have need." You don't say "need exists." You say "**I am needy**." You cry out to God along with David, who said "Yet I am poor and needy; come quickly to me, O God. You are my help and my deliverer; O Lord, do not delay" (Psalm 70:5). Your neediness isn't something that is separate from you—it's real, it's intimate, and it's immediate. You are needy for Him to come to you, to help you, and to deliver you. It's important to put it that way.

Now, as important as neediness is, the Bible doesn't say "need and you shall find." It specifically says "seek." It is possible to wallow in your neediness without seeking God. You can suffer about your circumstances without seeking new solutions. There's a name for that. That's called despair.

Needing isn't enough; you have to participate in your life by acknowledging your neediness and seeking Him through your experience of that neediness. You're not just complaining when you admit your neediness to

God. You are opening the door that motivates you to seek His aid.

I instructed Gary to get in touch with his need. I said, "Try this with me now: start some sentences with 'I am needy for You, O Lord, in my…' Then, from your heart, fill in the blanks about where you are hurting in your life. Keep repeating it, and notice what you start to experience."

"Okay," he said. "I'll try." He started out hurriedly, as if trying to get me off his back. "I am needy for You, O Lord, in my failing marriage. I am needy for You, O Lord, in my family. I am needy for You, O Lord, with my children."

But then he started slowing down. "I am needy, for You, O Lord, in my being a good husband." He paused, starting to really feel the truth of his neediness for God. "I am needy for You, O Lord, in being a loving and present father." Another pause. "I am needy for You, O Lord, in my bringing my family back together in love." His voice became hoarse with emotion. "I'm so needy right now, O Lord! I'm so needy!"

His neediness was present, and from that he began, automatically, to seek God with all his heart. But even as he expressed his neediness, I could hear the renewed optimism in his voice. Not a lot of it, but a start. God could touch his heart, because he was actually seeking

God **with** his heart. Gary was seeking God, not as a way of avoiding his life, but to help him **in** his life. He was on his way back.

How to Seek

I suggest you use the rhythm of your breath to guide you as you begin to seek God with all your heart. Here's how to do it:

OUT-BREATH: Silently or out loud, say "I am needy for You, O Lord, in my [whatever is upsetting you in your life]." Don't over-think this. The idea is to feel your neediness in your heart, and to speak from there as you exhale.

You are needy for God in the areas of your life that are difficult. In what circumstances of your life do you feel afraid, or angry, or sad, or ashamed, or alone? In what circumstances do you feel like you're not going to make it—or just barely make it if you do?

These are the circumstances of your life where you are most needy for God. And if you are going to seek God, and find Him, you must first feel that need.

You might begin to seek by saying,

> "I am needy for You, O Lord, in my staying close to You as I talk to my creditors."

"I am needy for You, O Lord, in my courageously handling the scary meeting I have today."

"I am needy for You, O Lord, in my having good humor as I get done what needs to be done today."

"I am needy for You, O Lord, in my being the best partner in the world for my spouse."

"I am needy for You, O Lord, in my having patience when my children interrupt me."

It may take more than one exhalation to state your need. That's okay. Take your time. Get honest about your need, and state it.

IN-BREATH: Silently say, "I am seeking You, O Lord." Experience how your need for God inspires you to seek Him. You may feel as if your heart is a compass, aligning you toward the "true north" of God. You may feel a sense of warmth. You may feel your heart move, or that light is starting to come to you. Whatever the feeling, let yourself experience it. (We'll more fully explore the idea of "experiencing" when we get to Gateway 3.)

Don't expect seeking to feel a certain way: The feeling of seeking God may be different every time you do it, every day, for the rest of your life. Simply align yourself with your seeking, and notice what you experience.

Try it Now

Don't be deceived by the simplicity of this exercise. When you repeat "I am needy for You, O Lord, in my…" you become present with your need. That need will motivate you to seek God—not as a "good idea," but in the way that a person underwater is motivated to seek air. When you acknowledge your neediness for God and seek Him from that need, you are participating in your life as your path for getting closer to Him. You are beginning the process of seeking God with all your heart and all your soul.

In a moment I'd like you to stop reading this book for, say, thirty seconds. During that time, on each out-breath repeat "I am needy for You, O Lord, in my…" and fill in the blank with whatever comes up from your needy heart. Then, on the in-breath, silently say "I am seeking You, O Lord," and "tune in" to your experience of your seeking.

Notice whatever inspiration to seek shows up for you. If nothing shows up, you might even say "I am needy for You, O Lord, in my seeking of You." Don't worry, just keep opening yourself in your need.

A couple of pointers:

MAKE THE EXERCISE ABOUT YOU. As best you can, stay away from "I am needy for You, O Lord, to change other people, or to change my circumstances." Move toward "I am needy for You, O Lord, in helping me become someone whose behavior is pleasing to You in the circumstances You have given me."

If you say "I am needy for You to fix this problem," or "I am needy for You to take this away," you are still not participating in the life God has given you—you are just wanting that life to go away. Instead, try to connect to your neediness for God to make you into what He desires you to become, in the face of your difficulties.

BE SPECIFIC ABOUT THE CIRCUMSTANCES. The more specific you are about what's upsetting you, the more connected you'll be to the need of your heart, and the more motivated you'll be to seek your Lord. If you say, "I am needy for You, O Lord, in my finances," you can still stay disconnected from your heart's neediness for God. Your motivation to seek Him will be weaker than it could be. But if you say "I am needy for You, O Lord, in my handling of my $248,000 in medical bills in the way You want me to," you will become emotionally present with your need for God, and that will strongly motivate your seeking.

DON'T WORRY IF YOUR NEED SEEMS TOO SMALL. No need is too small to take to God. Philippians 4:6 says, "In everything, by prayer and petition, with thanksgiving, present your requests to God." It doesn't say "just the big stuff." Bring to God whatever neediness is weighing on your heart right now, big or small. Though your need may be small, the grant from Him may be great. But you'll never know if you don't acknowledge the true need of your heart, large or small, and seek God with it.

Stop reading this for thirty seconds or so and try the exercise now.

What did you experience? If you are like Gary, you started to experience real, congruent, heart-based motivation to seek God. It will have felt real.

And you might have even started to feel His response to your seeking. You might have started to receive something in return.

And **receiving**, after **seeking**, is what we are exploring next.

Gateway Two: Receive

"When I think about Christ on the cross, I don't even know how to deal with it," Suzanna said. "He suffered and died for me! I just don't know how to relate to that kind of sacrifice."

Fifteen of us had come together for a weekend with the intention of exploring our relationships with God. The question Suzanna was answering was, "How do you relate to Christ's sacrifice for you?"

"Let's look into that," I suggested, "because you're bringing up an important question: When you don't know how to relate to Christ's sacrifice for you, what do you do?"

She grew silent. In fact, the whole room grew still as every person pondered his or her own answer to that question.

"Honestly," she said, "I guess I beat myself up about not being good enough for what Christ went through for me. Or I just check out and don't think about it at all. I know I shouldn't, but I just don't know how to relate to what God has given me. I really don't."

After she spoke I gave every person a chance to respond, and everyone identified with what she was saying. We were saved. Christ had paid the price for us. But even so, everyone had a lingering feeling of not being able to relate to Christ's sacrifice in any way that felt good.

A man named Jason said, "I know I should be living in the grace that Christ has provided, but I guess I'm like Suzanna—after everything he went through for me, I either feel guilty about it, which doesn't help, or I don't even think about it, which seems even worse. Most of the time I feel a little bad about Christ's suffering. It feels sort of like I have a low-grade fever all the time. I guess I also don't know how to relate to what Christ has given me."

"I Don't Know How to Relate to What Christ Has Given Me"

The gift of Christ's sacrifice has been given. That truth is not in question. The question is, how do you relate to that gift?

Most Christians do **not** relate to that gift by saying, "Wow! I can live every moment in the love and mercy that Christ's sacrifice has made available to me. That's wonderful! From now on, I'll refuse to accept anything less than living fully in the experience of that love and that mercy."

We **don't** do that.

Instead, we suffer with the "low-grade fever" of not knowing how to relate. Perhaps we give lip service to what Christ's sacrifice is supposed to mean. Or perhaps we feel guilty or "sort of bad" when we think about Christ on the cross. Or perhaps we forget about it entirely. But we don't really "live the gift" he's given us.

Because we don't know how.

Core Christian Mercy Number Two

The greatest signal of God's mercy is, "For God so loved the world that He gave His one and only Son" (John 3:16). God loved the world so much that He gave us His Son—even though our world was fallen, lost, and depraved—to wipe away our sin.

You may have a mountain of sins but God's love for you, expressed by His giving His Son, wipes them all away. You don't have to be burdened by your imperfection, now or ever, because "…it is by grace you have been saved, through faith—and this is not from yourselves, it is the gift of God" (Ephesians 2:8).

That gift is a mercy because it means:

> **You don't have to make up
> for your sins.**

As Christians, we are used to this idea. But I invite you now to allow yourself to join me in being shocked by it anew. Despite your humanity, despite your sinful nature, despite your screw-ups, despite your rebellion, despite your "missing the mark" in your attempts to be virtuous, you don't have to make up for your sins. You can live in the experience of God's grace, God's mercy, and God's love. He loves you that much. Every second of every day. Always. That's the gift of Christ's sacrifice.

And while you are absorbing that, I invite you to also notice, as did the people from my group, one other thing:

That gift can be really hard to relate to.

Balancing the Books

The gift of God's grace is hard to relate to because of the way you are wired:

You are wired to always try to "balance the books."

For instance…

- If someone gives you a gift, you are wired to want to "balance the books" by giving one back—and you'll feel uncomfortably out of balance until you do.

- If someone does you a favor, you are wired to want to "balance the books" by returning that favor—and you'll feel uncomfortably out of balance until you do.

- If you do something bad, or inconsiderate, or selfish, you are also wired to want to atone for your behavior—and you'll make yourself suffer until that "debt of atonement" is paid.

We don't like it when the give-and-take in our lives is unbalanced. That's our human nature. If we've taken more than we've given in return, we feel incomplete. We feel tense. We want to "set things right."

If you want to make sure that people will want to be around you, you've got to be a giver. We intuitively understand this, so we subconsciously keep track of what we owe to keep "the books" balanced with other people.

"Balancing the books" works well to keep human society together.

But it doesn't work with God.

Christ came to end the idea of "balancing the books" with God. That time is over. Christ ended it. We live in the time of grace.

But as I said, receiving without giving anything in return goes against the way our brains are wired. Receiving without giving goes against our human nature.

And because of that human nature, we unconsciously try to "balance the books" with God.

Christian Roadblock Number Two

Christian Roadblock number two is:

> **Christians try to get closer to God by "balancing the books" with Him.**

There are two ways we try to "balance the books" with God: We make ourselves suffer, in an attempt to repay Christ's sacrifice, or we push ourselves to be "good enough," in an attempt to be worthy of it.

Let's look at both methods:

"BALANCING THE BOOKS" BY MAKING YOURSELF SUFFER. Paradoxically, it's easier to suffer than it is to accept the gift God offers. So too often, we **don't** accept the gift of Christ's sacrifice by committing ourselves to living every day in the grace and the joy he made available to us. Instead, we try to balance Christ's suffering by making ourselves suffer, too.

We beat up on ourselves, unconsciously thinking something like, "Wow, if I wasn't so unworthy, Christ wouldn't have had to go through all that suffering for me. I am the reason he had to suffer so much. I should suffer to even the score." We then live with a "low-grade fever" of guilt and shame as we try to balance the books by suffering along with Christ.

"BALANCING THE BOOKS" BY TRYING TO BECOME WORTHY. If the books aren't balanced, we feel unworthy— which leads some of us to put off feeling God's love until we believe we are worthy. We unconsciously tell ourselves we'll be worthy later, once we've handled our sinful nature and are better Christians. But that "later" never comes. And until that ever-receding "later" arrives, we believe we have to work, alone and without God's love, to make ourselves worthy.

Some Christians also have another response, which isn't a way of trying to "balance the books" with God: **"checking out" entirely**. They relate to God's gift by not relating to it at all. Instead of attempting to balance their relationship with God, they run away from the problem.

Why would a person run away from such a gift? Well, consider this story:

A workshop participant once revealed that his wife had worked full-time to support him all the way through his medical school training.

Then, shortly after receiving his diploma, he left her.

He shared this experience after learning about "balancing the books." He said, "I know it was a terrible thing to do, but I felt like I **had to** leave. I didn't know why, but I felt **compelled**. And now I see I left because I couldn't accept how much she had given me. The more she gave to me, the more I felt like I'd never be able to make up for it. Then one day I just couldn't take it anymore. And I left." After years of receiving and receiving, the unbalanced nature of her sacrifice for him simply became too uncomfortable for him to bear, and he "checked out."

It's easy to judge this man harshly, but I consistently see believers who act **exactly the same way** regarding Christ's sacrifice for them. His gift is too overwhelming, so we check out. Like the man whose wife supported him through medical school, we find it too painful to face the magnitude of the gift that's been given to us. So we disengage.

"Balancing the Books" Gets in the Way of God's Gift

When you try to get closer to God by "balancing the books," you are blocking the very grace that Christ's sacrifice offers you. Jesus said, "I came that they may have life, and that they may have it more abundantly" (John 10:10). Your attempts to "settle your accounts" with God gets in the way of the abundant life that God wants you to have.

The truth is, God's grace is not transactional. When a human being does you a favor, you can "pay it back" and balance the books. But no matter how much you want to be close to God, you can't "pay back" the favor of His grace, His mercy and His love. No matter how hard you try, you'll never "balance the books" with God.

So many of us know this, but we unconsciously try to "balance the books" with God anyway. And when you try to balance your relationship with God, you get in the way of the life God wants to give you.

Christian Challenge Number Two

If Christians get in the way of the Lord's gift by trying to "balance the books," then the second Christian Challenge is:

To lay down your burden before God and
live in His love and mercy, in this
moment and in every moment of your life.

The challenge says, "Stop trying to balance your account with God. Stop trying to pay the price. Stop suffering to 'even things out.' Put down your burden and live in God's love and mercy, exactly as you are."

The Christian Challenge Is Hard

We need to let go of the idea that laying down your burden and living in the gift of God's love and mercy is a simple thing. It is not. Living in God's gift of love and mercy is hard. It sounds simple, until you try it. Then you discover it's a daily challenge.

Strange as it may sound, it's much more difficult to live a life of continuously experiencing God's love and mercy than it is to live a life of feeling bad about yourself and feeling guilty about Christ's sacrifice. Because imbalances are so intolerable to us, suffering to "balance the books" is actually easier than receiving God's gift. We are absolutely not used to living in love and mercy, especially not 100% of the time, as God offers. We are much more used to carrying the burden of our "low-grade fever" of guilt and shame. So that is how we live, leaving the actual experience of God's love until a never-arriving "later."

We have to learn to **receive** God's gift.

Gateway to God Number Two: Receive

Once you understand that you are trying to get closer to God by "balancing the books" with Him, you have a new option you didn't have before:

> Rather than suffering, trying to make yourself worthy, or checking out entirely, you can learn to receive the love that God expressed by sending His Son for you.

Let's get back to my group.

"Okay," I said. "We've noticed that we all tend to relate to God's gift to us by trying to 'balance the books' with Him. We sacrifice ourselves by feeling bad about ourselves, or we try to make ourselves good enough to be worthy of His gift. I'd like to walk you through an exercise to help with that."

1. FEEL THE BURDEN OF TRYING TO "BALANCE THE BOOKS" WITH GOD. I said, "I'd like you to close your eyes. Let yourself feel how you've tried to get close to God by 'balancing the books' for the gift he has given you.

"Feel the physical sensation of how hard it's been to try to live by 'balancing the books.' What's it like? That sensation might be like a weight you carry on your shoulders. It might be like a rock you've been struggling to hold in your arms. It could be anything. Let yourself discover how you feel when you try to 'balance the books' with God."

As you read this, imagine your own burden of trying to "balance the books" with God. Feel the weight of not allowing yourself to fully live in His grace. Experience the burden of feeling that you have to suffer to balance Christ's sacrifice, or that you have to put off receiving His mercy and love until you are good enough. Feel the weight of that burden now.

2. FEEL HOW WEARISOME THAT BURDEN IS. I gave my workshop attendees a moment, then continued. "Now," I said, "feel how wearisome it's been to try to get close to God by 'balancing the books.' Let yourself feel how weary you are from carrying that burden. Really feel it. It's been a hard way to live."

As you read this, let yourself feel how weary you are of carrying that burden. Really feel how exhausting it is to live without fully receiving God's mercy and love.

3. GO TO GOD WITH THAT BURDEN. I told the group, "Christ said, 'Come to me, all you who are weary and burdened.' Obey that instruction now. Imagine going to God with this wearisome burden of trying to 'balance the books' with Him."

As you read this, imagine yourself carrying your burden to God. Get your best sense of how it feels to show up, tired and burdened, before God.

4. LAY DOWN YOUR BURDEN BEFORE GOD. "Now," I told the group, "feel yourself before Him. Say to Him, 'My Lord, I have been carrying this burden in an attempt to 'balance the books' with You. I've made myself suffer because you suffered for me. I've pushed myself to 'do it right' for You. Or I've checked out entirely. This is the burden I've carried. This is what I've done instead of receiving from You.'"

I gave them a moment to experience that, then continued. "Now remember, Psalm 55:22 tells us, "Cast your cares on the Lord, and He will sustain you." Let's do that now. Imagine taking that burden in your arms, and laying it before your Lord. Really let yourself feel what it's like to put that burden down before Him, to 'cast your cares on the Lord.'"

As you read this, take a moment to tell God about the burden you've carried. Tell Him what it's been like to feel that you have to suffer to make up for Christ's suffering, or that you have to make yourself better before you can accept His love, or that you have to check out entirely. Share with Him, from your heart.

Then take that burden, and lay it down before God. As best you can, cast that care on the Lord. Experience what it's like to let go of it, and to give it to Him.

5. FEEL THE LOVE THAT THE HEART OF GOD HAS FOR YOU. I said, "Now open yourself up to the love that God must have for you, to want to take your burden, to want to give you love and mercy, to want to give you grace. Open yourself up to the heart of God. Begin to focus on the love God has for you, a love that He expressed by giving so much for you." I let the group experience that for a few moments. Several participants opened their arms wide, as if experiencing a deep feeling. Everyone seemed at peace.

As you read this, let yourself tune into your best sense of the love that would motivate God to give so much for you. Let yourself focus on that love. Let yourself receive from that love in God's heart.

6. ASK, "DOES GOD WANT YOU TO TRY TO 'BALANCE THE BOOKS?'" I continued: "Now let yourself discover your best sense of the answer to this question: Does God really want you to relate to His gift by 'balancing the books' with Him? Does He want you to suffer, or to try to make yourself 'good enough' for His gift?

48

Does He want you to 'check out' because you have a hard time relating to what He wants to give you? Get your best sense of the answer to that question, now."

As you read, do the same. "Listen" with openness in your heart, and get your best, emotional sense of His answer to these questions:

- Does God want you to suffer and feel guilty because Christ suffered?

- Does God want you to put off feeling His grace until you finally "get it right"?

- Does God want you to "check out," and not experience His love and mercy?

- Does God want you to try to "balance the books" with Him?

7. RECEIVE WHAT HE GIVES YOU. "Remember," I told the group, "Christ didn't stop at, 'Come to me all who are weary and burdened.' He also said, 'I will give you rest.' If God doesn't want you to try to pay Him back for His gift, then how might He want you to live? And how might that way of living be restful for the weary part of you that has carried this burden? Receive that, now."

As you read this, allow yourself to feel whatever you receive from the love God has for you. Don't worry if you aren't receiving "perfectly." Just try it, even a little bit. Once you get a taste of how to receive, you'll get better at it with each repetition.

Opening the Gateway of Receiving from God

After this exercise, I asked people to share what they had received. "I just felt like I received relief," Suzanna said. "I've been trying so hard to be good enough for God, and this experience showed me that I could stop doing that. Once I lay down that burden before Him, I got the light, the joy, the peace, the relief. I really feel like I have permission to live in the light of His gift. That's the 'rest' I received."

"I felt like I had His favor," a man offered. "That's the best way to put it. He favors me in my heart, and favors what I choose to pursue in my life. I felt Him sustaining me through life. It felt so good."

"For me," another woman shared, "it felt like that feeling of summertime when I was a kid. That feeling of freedom, that feeling of infinite possibility. I haven't felt that way in years. I saw that so much more is possible for me than I've been believing."

Finally Jason, the man who'd said he felt like he had a "low-grade fever," spoke up. "I felt like God was telling me that I am a good man, and I should never forget it, no matter what is going on. I can let go of that guilt and dwell in the goodness He's put into me. I can receive from Him. It's wonderful."

The people in my group had experienced a shift. They opened themselves to receiving from the heart of God that loved them so much that He would sacrifice for them, wait for them, and always extend mercy to them. And from that deep sense of God's love, they had received new guidance about how they could experience the gift of God.

Now It's Your Turn

If you didn't try the exercise while you were reading it, you might want to go back and give it a shot now. If you did try it, what happened?

We each carry many burdens that we would do well to give to God. Trying to "balance the books" with Him for His gift is only one of them. There may be some other burden you've been carrying that it's time for you to let go of. You can use this exercise to lay down that burden before God, and to discover what you receive from Him when you do so.

Once you've begun **receiving** from God, you are ready for the next step: living in the **experience** of the love you receive from Him.

Gateway Three: Experience

Imagine you are driving through a desert. It's a hot day, the black pavement scorched by the blasting sun. You see a hiker staggering by the side of the road, and you stop to offer your help.

One look shows you that he's long overdue for a drink of water. His skin is pale, his lips cracked, his eyes glazed over.

You offer him a drink from your water bottle, but he waves it away. "I don't need water," he tells you thickly. "You see, I've made this list of the ways a person who isn't thirsty would behave." He produces a notepad and shows you a meticulously written checklist: "Be relaxed. Stand tall. Have abundant energy. Glow with health. Exude joy. Smile." Through cracked lips he tells you, "If I just do what's on this list, I'll be fine."

It's easy to see that this hiker has the situation exactly backwards. You don't overcome thirst by becoming more skillful at acting as if you are not thirsty. You overcome thirst by drinking water. You might even tell this dehydrated hiker, "Stop trying to act as if your thirst is quenched! Take my water bottle and drink!"

Core Christian Mercy Number Three

There's a saying that you can never step into the same river twice: A river is constantly renewed, because the water is always moving. Every time you step into a river, you have a brand-new experience of it. The water you stepped into before is long gone, and new flowing waters have taken its place.

That kind of flowing, always-new, ever-changing experience may be what Jesus is talking about when he speaks of the "water" that he provides:

> "If anyone thirsts, let him come to me and drink. Whoever believes in me, as the Scripture has said, 'Out of his heart will flow rivers of living water.'" (John 7:37-38)

> "If you knew the gift of God and who it is that asks you for a drink, you would have asked him and he would have given you living water." (John 4:10)

> "Whoever drinks the water I give them will never thirst. Indeed, the water I give them will become

in them a spring of water welling up to eternal life." (John 4:14)

The gift of God, then, is "living water": an ever-abundant source that we can step into and drink from at any time. And because "God is love" (1 John 4:8), and Christ gives us living water, that tells us something about a core Christian mercy:

> God's love is a living, flowing experience.

God's love flows, and the experience of that love is never exactly the same twice. His love is always a new river, a different experience, every time you connect with it. Like a river of living water, like an ever-flowing spring, God's love is a living, flowing experience.

Christian Roadblock Number Three

Let's get back to our thirsty desert hiker. It's easy to see that his "checklist-based" approach of pretending he's not thirsty will never bring him joy, peace, or health. No matter how well he performs the behaviors on his checklist, it's easy to see that those behaviors will never quench his thirst.

But all too often I see Christians take the same approach to Christianity as that hiker takes to thirst. That's the third Christian Roadblock:

Christians try to get closer to God by making Christianity into a checklist.

Instead of drinking from the living waters of God's love, "Checklist Christians" focus on fulfilling a check-list of the behaviors they would naturally perform **if** they were drinking of God's love. They make being a "good Christian" into the practice of checking boxes off of the Christian Checklist.

Now, checklists are important for us. They provide guideposts for our faith, for our actions, and for our hearts. There is nothing wrong with having checklists. The problem comes when checklists become substi-tutes for for the living, flowing experience of God that they are meant to guide us toward.

Items on the Christian Checklist fall into three main categories:

A "GOOD CHRISTIAN" PROFESSES THE RIGHT THINGS. While they may vary from denomination to denomi-nation, some items on a "profess-the-right-things" checklist might include: Profess the divinity of Christ. Profess that Jesus is the savior. Profess to believe in the Holy Trinity. Profess that the Bible is the literal word of God. Profess to believe in the virgin birth. Profess to believe the Nicene and Apostles' Creeds.

A "GOOD CHRISTIAN" DOES THE RIGHT THINGS. While those actions may vary from denomination to denomination, some items on a "do-the-right-things" checklist might include: Study the Bible for an hour every day. Give generously. Always wear a smile (at least at church). Never say anything negative. Never let anyone see you having problems with yourself, your life or your family. Never miss church. Never express doubt. Never swear or lose your temper. Pray for the world.

A "GOOD CHRISTIAN" FEELS THE RIGHT THINGS AND DOES NOT FEEL THE WRONG THINGS. While those emotions may vary from denomination to denomination, some items on a "feel-the-right-things" checklist might include: Always be happy. Always be forgiving. Don't feel inappropriate sexual feelings. Always feel joyful and grateful, not sad or upset about life's difficulties. Always feel loving toward all, never angry or irritated. Never feel fear, but feel only trust in God's plan.

If you allow fulfilling the Christian Checklist to become the goal of your spiritual life, you'll no longer experience the living, flowing nature of God's love. You'll miss out on the waters that God offers you.

Making Christianity into a Checklist Substitutes Appearance for Experience

When you make Christianity into a checklist, you substitute appearing as if you are not thirsty for actually having your thirst quenched. You substitute appearance for experience.

In other words:

- Making Christianity into a checklist is like going to a fine restaurant and spending your entire visit looking at the menu.

- Making Christianity into a checklist is like taking a vacation at a world-class resort and spending it sitting in your room looking at postcards of the local attractions.

- Making Christianity into a checklist is like driving to the head of a magnificent hiking trail and sitting in your car looking at a map of the territory.

Fulfilling checklist items is not the same as having the experiences those items represent. You did go to the restaurant (check!). But you didn't eat. You did visit the resort (check!). But you didn't see the sights. You did drive to the hiking trail (check!). But you didn't feel it underfoot. You can check items off your list, but you didn't have the living, flowing experiences those items represent. Living from a checklist, rather than from the experience itself, makes your experiences static and lifeless.

Making Christianity into a checklist has the same result. It takes the experience of God's love—which is inherently living and flowing—and makes it into boxes on a checklist, behaviors for you to perform through effort and willpower. Making Christianity into a checklist dams the "rivers of living water" and caps the "welling springs." Like the thirsty hiker with his checklist, you may **appear** to "do the right things," but you won't **experience** having your thirst quenched. You may **look** right, but you won't **be** right.

Christian Challenge Number Three

I was surprised to learn that desert hikers have sometimes been found dead from dehydration, even though they had canteens of water with them. These hikers knew the importance of having access to water, but they did not fully understand that they needed to **drink** that water, too.

I started to understand how a hiker could die of thirst while carrying water when I realized that something similar happens to "Checklist Christians." Just as you can have a full bottle of water and not drink from it, it's possible to have the living water of God's love available to you and not experience it. After all, knowing the water is available is not enough; you have to drink. When you try instead to fulfill the Christian Checklist, you can die of spiritual thirst with a full canteen on your belt.

And that leads us to the third Christian challenge:

> To drink deeply of the living,
> flowing waters of God's love.

Again: It's not enough to make lists of the qualities you would have if you drank that water, and to try to act as if you had them. It's not even enough to acknowledge those waters are available.

You actually have to drink.

Effort is Important

Of course, making effort toward behaving well is important. Jesus said, "If you love me, keep my commandments" (John 14:15). You have to **try** to be virtuous. Paul says that you are to "…work out your salvation with fear and trembling" (Philippians 2:12). You have to make effort toward doing well.

But effort alone is not enough. If it were, then you wouldn't need the living waters of God's love: your effort, your "doing good works," would eliminate your need for God.

Effort is important because it is a sign of your participation in your life. But the source of your virtue is not your own effort. The source of your virtue is the spirit of God working within you—the living waters of God's love that nourish your heart.

If "fulfilling the Christian checklist" is your main goal, then it will be as hard for you to behave virtuously as it is for that desert hiker to behave as if he is not thirsty. That "good behavior" may be possible, but it will be incredibly challenging to maintain. And people will think that your pious virtue is forced and insincere.

Yes, you must try to behave well. But if you want to succeed at behaving well, you must also accept the challenge of drinking deeply of the living, flowing waters of God's love.

The Christian Challenge is Hard

God is infinite, and we are very small. And because of His infinite nature, God's love can show up differently for you every time you experience it. In fact, He could give you a completely new experience of His love in every instant of existence from now through all of eternity. He's that big.

That means you have to constantly be alert for how God's love is showing up for you **right now.** Simply trying to replay the way His love appeared for you previously won't work, because your experience of God's love keeps changing.

You've got to **wake up** and be **fully aware** if you want to experience what God has for you. You can't say, "I'll just do a replay of what He gave me yesterday" because, well, "He makes all things new." Over and over. Forever. Every time you open to experiencing what He's giving you, you have to be **fully alert** for a fresh and new experience. It's a whole new river. You can't step into the same one twice.

And that's difficult. Whether we like to admit it or not, many of us prefer our lives to be familiar. Many of us would prefer to keep traveling the well-worn ruts of our routines, and to keep checking items off of our checklists.

On the other hand, continuously rediscovering the living, flowing experience of God's love is much more fulfilling than living that routine, checklist-based existence. It's a daily, moment-by-moment rediscovering of delight in God's love.

But don't kid yourself. It is challenging.

Gateway to God Number Three: Experience

In the first gateway you learned to **seek** by acknowledging your need. In the second gateway you discovered how to open to **receiving** what you sought for in Gateway One.

But it does you little good to **receive** love from God if you don't actually know how to **experience** what you are receiving. Psalm 34:8 says, "Taste and see that the Lord is good." "Tasting and seeing" is not intellectual. It's **experiential**. Tasting is putting the waters of God's love into your mouth, and feeling for yourself what the experience is like. Experiencing is real, immediate, and visceral.

Opening the Gateway of Experiencing God's Love

Experiencing God's love is a spiritual discipline you have to develop. And like any skill, good instruction helps, and practice is essential.

Experiencing God's love always starts with **seeking** Him with all your heart. Remember the exercise from Gateway One: You seek by confessing your neediness to God, and by stating your intention to seek for Him. On your out-breath you say, "I am needy for You, O Lord, in [something that's upsetting you in your life]," and on the in-breath you silently say, "I am seeking You, O Lord." That simple exercise activates your seeking for God—not just in your head, but with the neediness of your heart.

Once your seeking is activated, you will often discover that you begin **receiving** automatically. That's because God wants to give to you. Remember again, Jesus said, "I came that they may have life, and have it abundantly" (John 10:10). He wants you to be in that abundant state of receiving. If you're having trouble starting to receive, it's probably because you are carrying the burden of trying to "balance the books" with God for everything He's given you. Lay that burden down before Him, and receive permission to release it and to receive His love (the exercise from Gateway Two).

But, as I've said, receiving is not enough if you don't **experience** what you receive. It's not enough to be given a canteen of water. You have to drink from it, or you can die of thirst with it strapped to your belt. And you "drink" of God's love through your senses, your emotions, and your insights.

Experiencing God's Love Through Your Senses, Your Emotions, and Your Insights

You may hesitate to trust the sensations of your body because your body can so easily lead you astray. But even so, when God guides you, you **sense** it, so it's appropriate to use your system of sensation—your body—to experience what He has for you. That's not wrong. What's wrong is to turn your sensory systems toward any source other than Him, and to receive through your body any spirit other than God. When you turn your alertness to God, however, your entire body can act as an antenna, receiving the signals of His love and guidance.

Experiencing what you receive from God is not automatic, and it's especially not automatic for people who've been trying to live their lives from a Christian checklist. Fortunately, there are three steps you can take to help you experience the living waters of God's love.

After you've begun your seeking, try these three steps to "turn on" your experiencing. While there are no hard-and-fast rules, I've found that people usually get the best results by following these steps in this order:

STEP 1: Ask yourself, "How am I experiencing what I'm receiving from God, as a sensation in my body?" When you **seek** God using the exercise from Gateway One you will usually begin **receiving**, and the first sign that you are receiving will usually be a sensation in your body. You need to draw your attention to that sensation by asking yourself, "How am I **experiencing** what I'm receiving from God, as a sensation in my body?"

For example, you may begin to feel a sense of warmth in your chest. Or you may feel as though you are being bathed in light. You might feel you are being lifted up, or that you can lean back and that there is something there to support you. Or you might feel that you are standing on firmer ground, or that you are somehow taller.

There is no set way you may sense this. As I mentioned before, your experience of God can be different every time you experience Him, every day, for the rest of your life. Many people experience warmth, or a sense of light in their bodies, but it varies. I've worked with a man who felt God's love as "a vague relaxation in my shoulders," with a woman who felt "like I am galloping with wild horses," and yet another man who said, "It feels like my body is a sail, and God is the wind filling me up."

STEP 2: Ask, "Do these sensations in my body seem like any particular emotion?" In this step you may begin to get a sense of the emotion or emotions that God feels about you. "I don't know the answer to my problems," a person at this step might say, "but this warmth I feel seems like God's love for me." Or a person at this step might say, "This sensation I'm experiencing is actually God-given joy. I still have the same situations in my life, but I feel peaceful and happy."

Warning: Don't skip over or rush through these steps. Take some time to experience the sensation of the flow in your body, and drink deeply of these good feelings. Let the shower of God's love pour down upon you, and experience it in whatever way you experience it.

STEP 3: Ask, "What does this emotion say to me about my life?" As you experience the new sensation in your body (step 1) and start to emotionally experience your best sense of how God feels about you (step 2), you will naturally start to think differently about your life. When you ask yourself "What does this emotion say to me about my life?," new insights and new guidance may appear.

In this step people say things like,

> "Wow, I thought I was caught in the middle, but now I see I'm a bridge to peace."

> "I thought everything was going down the drain, but now I see it truly is a new beginning."

> "I thought God was giving me hard times for no reason, but now I see He's knocking the rocks off my wings so I can fly."

"I thought I was a dried-out husk, but now I see that God's love has hydrated me, and I'm enlarged and supported in whatever I choose to do."

"I thought the demands of life were crushing me, but now I see I only have to handle one moment at a time."

These three questions open the gateway of **experiencing** whatever transmission God has for you.

Online Extra: "But He's Not There!"

In this online extra, I give some guidance for the times you might try to experience what God has for you, but instead find yourself experiencing your anger or disappointment about how God has treated you. It's a trap Christians sometimes fall into in which they end up saying, "I'm trying to receive from Him, but He's not there!" Read about it at

GatewaysToGod.com/experiencing

Through a Mirror, Dimly

The idea of receiving insights from the experience of God's love brings up an important question: How can you know for certain that the insight you think you are receiving from God is actually what He is intending for you?

The answer is that you can't. Paul tells us, "For now we see in a mirror, dimly" (1 Corinthians 13:12). We only see only a dim reflection of God's love, as if in a mirror. We don't get a full and perfect view of it, the way we will when we see it later, as Paul says, "face to face."

When you experience insight and guidance from God, it's important to remember that you see a dim reflection of God, which may distort what you are receiving. Just because you might feel convinced that you fully understand God's message for you doesn't mean that you actually do. You might be wrong. The mirror is dim.

Or to make the point in a more contemporary way, I'd like to quote advice columnist Miss Manners, who once said, "Letters explaining God's opinions should not be written." The same is true anytime you speak with certainty about the guidance you experience from God's love. You don't speak for God, and you don't know His opinion.

But that doesn't mean you can't benefit from your best sense of your experience of God's love, or that you can't receive guidance from God, or that you can't experience closeness with God. You absolutely can. But remain humble in your knowledge that the mirror is dim and your vision is not absolutely clear.

Experience What You Receive from God, Not What You Receive from Your Brain

Please note: You are unlikely to have new insights if you don't first experience the living, flowing nature of God's love, both through your senses and through your emotions. That's because experiencing through your senses and through your emotions makes your experience real. If you skip experiencing through your senses and through your emotions, you'll be tempted to turn instead to your own smart brain. After all, your brain can give you plenty of insights about what you "should" think — generally along the lines of "God has a plan," or "all things are possible with God." But those "insights" won't surprise and delight you. They won't feel like peace, or joy, or relief. They'll feel like what they are: good advice about what you should — but aren't able to — be like. As such, they end up just being more items for your checklist.

Insights born of drinking God's love generally arrive on a current of sensation and emotion, in much the way a leaf rides a current down a river, or a surfer rides a wave toward shore. If you skip the steps of experiencing through your senses and through your emotions, then you'll be like that thirsty hiker with his checklist of behaviors. You may be acting in the proper manner. But you'll be thirsty inside.

Experiencing in Your Secret Heart

In Psalm 51:6, David says to God, "Behold, You delight in truth in the inward being, and You teach me wisdom in the secret heart." If you want to experience what you receive from God, you're going to have to do some exploration of your inward being. That means you are going to have to **experience** what He puts into your secret heart. In this chapter I've shared my favorite way to do that.

Now that you understand **seeking**, **receiving**, and **experiencing**, it's time for the next gateway: **being made new** by what you experience from God.

Gateway Four:
Be Made New

"I'm just so attracted to college girls," Sam told me. "I know I shouldn't look at them, but I can't help myself. I'm out in public and I steal glances at their bodies. They know it, I'm sure. It makes me feel really bad about myself. And it probably isn't so great for them, either."

A married 55-year-old man, Sam had come to me complaining that he had repented, but nothing had changed. He still kept finding himself looking with lust at young women.

"When you repented, what did you do?" I asked. "Walk me through it, step by step."

"Okay," he said. "I had been out running errands, and I stopped at a coffee shop down by the university, and there they were—all these beautiful young women. I couldn't help myself. I don't think I gaped openly, but I definitely looked. I felt guilty about it, so when I got back to my car, I decided to repent. I basically told God everything I had done — not like He didn't already know, but still. I told Him I felt bad about looking at these women with lust, and I asked Him to forgive me for what I had done and to lift this behavior from me."

"So how did that go?" I asked.

"Honestly? Not so well. I still felt bad, but I was hopeful God would change me in the future. But wouldn't you know it, just an hour later I was at the hardware store, and I ended up checking out the young woman behind the cash register. As usual, my repentance hadn't done anything for me. My behavior hadn't improved. Truthfully, I sometimes think it would be easier if I didn't repent at all. When I repent I just feel worse."

Core Christian Mercy Number Four

In the first gateway, we saw the transformational mercy of "God's love is with you in every moment." In the second gateway, we realized the profound beauty and relief of knowing "You don't have to make up for your sins." In Gateway Three we felt the uplifting and energizing mercy that "God's love is a living, flowing experience." Now, the fourth mercy.

Since becoming Christian, I've been greatly comforted knowing that I am forgiven for any sin. But the comfort goes deeper than that. Consider these two examples of God's mercy:

> "If anyone is in Christ, he is a new creation. The old has passed away; behold, the new has come." (2 Corinthians 5:17)

> "As far as the east is from the west, so far has He removed our transgressions from us." (Psalm 103:12)

As I reflected on such verses I saw that the core mercy of Roadblock four is:

> **God's forgiveness makes you a new creation, every single time.**

You are not just forgiven—you can be made into a new creation. Isaiah tells us to "Forget the former things; do not dwell on the past...I am making a way in the wilderness and streams in the wasteland" (Isaiah 43:18-19). A way can be made through the "impassable wilderness" of your life. Streams of renewal can flow through what you once thought was a wasteland of incorrigible sin. You don't have to dwell in the past. Through Him all things can be made new.

That's pretty inspiring.

But if that's so true, then why was my client having such a hard time changing his behavior? And why do so many other Christians seem to be unchanged by repentance?

Getting Some "R&R"

The word "repentance" comes from a Greek word that means "a change of mind and heart" or "a change of consciousness."

In Hebrew, the idea of repentance means both "to feel sorrow" and "to return." You repent by first feeling remorse about what you've done (the sorrow), and then by returning to God for a change of mind, heart, and consciousness. Repentance is all about "Remorse and Return." I call it "R&R" for short.

If you want repentance to change your heart and change your behavior, you've got to get that R&R.

Christian Roadblock Number Four

Christians are really good at the first "R"—we feel tremendous Remorse for our sins. But we often can't quite get to the second "R" of Returning to God and being changed. Like my client who kept lusting after young women, Christians often get to the point of suffering remorse, but don't go any further. They just keep suffering.

For so many of the Christians I work with, this is precisely the problem:

> Christians try to get closer to God
> by suffering through repentance.

When we stop with remorse and don't return to God to be changed, we stop the process in the middle. We suffer, but we are not made new. We stay discouraged and stuck with our sinning behaviors.

Why Would You Stop with Remorse?

It's one thing to try to repent once and not be changed. But it's another thing to try a dozen times, or a hundred times, and still not be changed. When that happens, what's a Christian to do?

That's when Christians give up. After failing repeatedly at having their sinful behaviors changed through repentance, they unconsciously conclude that, when it comes to changing those behaviors, God isn't really there for them. They give up on returning to God to be changed.

Sam himself felt that way. "I guess that after all this try-ing," he told me, "I'm just stuck with my sinning nature. I still feel bad about it, but I feel like I'm on my own." Once you've given up on God changing you, as Sam had, there is no "R&R." There is no returning to God to be for a change of mind, heart, and consciousness. There's only the pain of remorse.

If returning to God to remove our sin doesn't seem like an option, then we have little choice but to turn to ourselves. And when we turn to ourselves to over-come our sin, we always take the same approach: instead of experiencing God's mercy, we become harsh with ourselves.

And when harshness doesn't stop our sinning—and it never does, not for long—we feel even more remorse, and become even more harsh with ourselves. It's a vicious cycle that feeds on itself and keeps us from truly going to God.

Christian Challenge Number Four

The fourth Christian challenge is:

> To keep returning to God
> until you are remade.

God has promised that "I will give you a new heart and put a new spirit in you; I will remove from you your heart of stone and give you a heart of flesh" (Ezekiel 36:26). But if you only feel the remorse for your sins, and give up on returning to God to change them, then that promise never gets a chance to come true.

If you stop with remorse you never get that "heart of flesh." You end up struggling through life with a heart of stone.

Online Extra

Read a story about repentance and "the low door to heaven" in this online extra. It's at

GatewaysToGod.com/door

The Christian Challenge of Returning to God is Hard

The Bible says "Ask, and ye shall receive." Yet for so many of us, if God doesn't give us what we ask for pretty quickly, we stop asking. But Scripture doesn't say "Ask until you get tired of asking, then give up." It says "ask." When Christians stop with the remorse, we stop asking.

Continuing to ask God to remake you is hard. It doesn't "just happen." Experiencing the joy of returning to God and being remade requires daily practice. It requires asking again and again.

And living that way is challenging.

We need to let go of the idea that just because we are called to return to God and be made new, that therefore that process is easy. It's not. It's actually easier to suffer in remorse, and to keep beating ourselves up about our sins, than it is to keep returning to God to be remade.

After all, beating ourselves up is our default human behavior. Mercilessness is what we're used to. So it's difficult to let go of that familiar pattern and return to God. And it's especially hard when we don't get the transformation we are looking for on the schedule that we would prefer. It's easier to give up, get in the driver's seat yourself, and scold, shame, and otherwise try to fix your sins yourself. That's the strategy Sam had tried. The problem is, it never really works.

Instead we need to open the gateway of **being made new.**

Gateway to God Number Four:
Be Made New

In the first gateway I shared how acknowledging your need for God is the gateway that helps you **seek** Him. In the second gateway we discovered how to open the gateway of **receiving** from God by connecting with the love He has for you that motivated Him to send His Son. In the third gateway we explored turning your body, your emotions and your insights to God to help you **experience** the living, flowing nature of His love.

The fourth gateway is to **be made new** by your experience of that love. Isaiah says, "Behold, I will create new heavens and a new earth. The former things will not be remembered, nor will they come to mind" (Isaiah 65:17). Being made new is about forgetting the former things and experiencing life in a new way—a way that is so much better than the old way that the sinful behavior is not remembered and doesn't come to mind.

The point of repentance isn't for us to be good Christian boys and girls or to learn to somehow survive without our "guilty pleasures." Nor is the point of repentance to give us some sort of "consolation prize" to take the place of the behaviors we really want to act out.

It may take time, but when God is done with you in repentance—when you have really been made new by His mercy and His love—you won't even feel tempted to act out the sin again. Doing so would feel like "going backwards." The old will have been forgotten. You will have been made new.

Being Made New Can't Be Faked

Being made new can't be faked. The process requires that you let go of trying to look good because you "did repentance right," or of trying to look good because you were instantly made new. Being made new will take as long as it takes, and you're going to have to go back to God to be made new until the transformation is complete.

That transformation may very well be complete the first time you ask to be remade—I always repent with that prayer in my heart—but it might not, and you have to be willing to seek, receive, experience and be made new by God as often as it takes.

So what if you ask and still aren't made new? It's not a sign that you are bad. It's not an occasion to be harsh with or to shame yourself. It's simply a sign that you need more forgiveness, more love, and more mercy in your heart. "For I know the plans I have for you, declares the Lord, plans to prosper you and not to harm you, plans to give you hope and a future" (Jeremiah 29:11). It's like the T-shirt says: "Be patient. God isn't finished with me yet." If you still aren't made new, be patient—you simply aren't finished being made into what God is planning to make you into.

Opening the Gateway of Being Made New

Because we Christians often get stuck in the remorse part of repentance, it's helpful to have a step-by-step exercise to take you through the process of **remorse** to **returning** to **being made new**.

I'll illustrate this exercise with an example of sin from my own life, and then with my client Sam, whom I spoke of at the start of this chapter.

First, the example of my sin. When I arise in the morning, my first activity is to spend time in prayer and remembrance of God. But for some weeks, I'd been having a problem: Instead of praying, I was ignoring my time with God and goofing off on the Internet before finally starting to pray. Turning to the Internet instead of turning to God was not the most inspired way I could imagine starting my day. But that's what I was doing, and I wanted to stop.

Here's the step-by-step process I used to give myself some "R&R" so I could be made new by God:

STEP 1: Ask yourself, "What is it costing me to act out this sin?" The first step of going from **remorse** to

returning is to understand the price you pay, in your life right now, for acting out your sin. One hint: make sure you discover the cost to you, not only the cost to other people, or to God, of your sinful behavior. "It hurts my spouse's feelings" might truly be a result of your sin, but the question here is: What is the cost of that result, to you? Is it that your spouse no longer trusts you or treats you with disdain? While external consequences are important, if you want to be motivated to return to God, you cannot ignore the cost of your sin to **you**.

When I turned to the Internet first thing in the morning rather than turning to God, it cost me my experience of God's support. I went into my day feeling as if I were "going at it alone."

STEP 2: Feel your heartbreak about being stuck with the cost of your sin. Understanding the cost of your sin intellectually is not enough. You also have to feel the cost emotionally, in your heart. If you don't feel the cost emotionally, that cost won't be real to you. And if the cost isn't real to you, you won't have the urgent motivation you'll need to return to God.

Psalm 34:18 says, "The Lord is close to the broken-hearted, and saves those who are crushed in spirit." It doesn't say, "The Lord is close to those who think a lot about their sin." He is close to those who are "crushed in spirit"—those who are emotionally involved in their lives enough to know the brokenheartedness that their sin engenders. Understanding the cost of your sin is important (step 1), but you have to **feel** that cost, as well. Whether the sin you are repenting of seems big or small, whether it seems "heartbreaking" or merely unfortunate, in order for it to be real for you, you have to feel the cost.

I felt my heartbreak in turning to the Internet instead of turning to God: "I'm heartbroken," I admitted. "I feel like I have to go through life without God's love. That hurts."

STEP 3: Ask yourself, "What do I feel like I get out of this sinful behavior that I'd have a hard time doing without?" One of the reasons we have such difficulty stopping our sinful behavior is because, unconsciously, we believe that the sinful behavior is giving us some benefit we would have a hard time doing without.

I'm not suggesting that you need your sin or that your sin has benefits. I'm saying that you hang onto your sin because you **perceive** that you need it and because you **perceive** that it has benefits. Some part of you believes that you get something from your sinful behavior that you would have a hard time doing without. And until that false belief is addressed, you will have a very hard time whole-heartedly returning to God to be made new.

Until you admit that you believe you get something you seem to need from your sinful behavior, you will unconsciously resist going to God to be remade — after all, who would want to be remade, if being remade meant having to live without something that you need?

When I asked myself "What do I feel like I get out of this sinful behavior that I'd have a hard time doing without?," I realized that I felt as if the time I spent browsing the Internet was "a time just for me," a window of freedom from all my responsibilities. And frankly, that window of freedom — that time just for me — felt like something I would have had a hard time doing without.

STEP 4: Notice the impossible choice you are faced with. It's as if you are faced with an impossible choice: either you can sin and have what you feel like you need, or you can choose not to sin, but do without the thing you feel like you need. Given those alternatives, it doesn't matter how strongly you vow not to sin anymore. If it seems like your sinful behavior is giving you something you need, you'll inevitably return to it. You need what you need, and your drive for it will eventually overwhelm your resolve to behave differently.

For me, I realized that I believed I was stuck with this impossible choice: Either I could turn to the Internet and ignore God, or I could go to God but live without a responsibility-free time just for me. Both options felt heartbreaking.

STEP 5: Go to God with the question, "Is this choice really true?" Now it's time to return to God by going to Him with the question, "Is this choice really true?" Are you really stuck with either choosing to sin to get what you need, or choosing not to sin but doing without what you need?

Be aware: There's a difference between asking God "Is this choice really true?" and asking your own smart brain the same question. Your brain will give you the "right" answer—"it's not true"—right away. But if you go to your own brain for the answer, you won't feel the emotional truth of that answer, and you won't be changed. Remember in the last chapter, when I talked about how you have to **experience** what God gives you—first through your **senses**, then through your **emotions**, and finally through your **thoughts and insights**. You have to follow that same sequence when you turn to God with the question "Is this choice really true?"

I began **seeking** God's answer to my conundrum—my belief that I was trapped with an impossible choice—by feeling my need for Him the way a person underwater feels his or her need for air. I said "I am needy for You, O Lord, to know if I'm really stuck with the choice of sinning or doing without time for me."

As I sought God with this question, I started **receiving** and **experiencing**. First I felt a softness come into my limbs and a sense of light come into my upper body. I gave myself time to be filled up by the physical sensations of that experience.

After a time I asked myself, "If this sensation was an emotion, what might that emotion be?" I realized that the softness and light felt like the joy of clemency, the joy of forgiveness from God. I let myself bask in that joy as the clemency and forgiveness filled me up.

I had experienced what God was giving me in my **body** (with the sensations of softness and light), and in my **emotions** (with the joy of His clemency and forgiveness). The next step was to ask myself if this experience crystallized into any sort of new **insight** about my supposedly being stuck with an impossible choice.

From those feelings of joy and release I began to see my "impossible choice" differently. I realized that I could easily and joyously wake up in the morning and slide right into my prayer time. I saw how my prayer time lifts me up and welcomes me to it. The transition from waking to prayer felt easy and natural.

I began to see that my morning prayer time wasn't a chore; instead it was a time of experiencing the certainty that everything is in God's hands, and of feeling the freedom that came along with that certainty. My prayer time was, in fact, a beautiful, responsibility-free time "just for me."

This new insight wasn't just some sort of "consolation prize" I got in exchange for giving up my sin. That beautiful time with God was something I truly wanted, much more than I wanted to noodle around on the Internet. There was no contest in the competition between what God offered me in my prayer time and what the Internet offered me during that same period. I emphatically wanted the prayer.

STEP 6: Notice how you are remade as a new creation. When you imagine yourself in the situation where you used to sin, what is different now? You'll know you are made new when the idea of acting out the sinful behavior no longer makes sense to you on an emotional level, not just on an intellectual one.

After I did this exercise, I could easily imagine getting up in the morning and sliding right into prayer. And, in fact, that's how I've been living ever since.

I was made new.

Online Extra: Knowing There Is a Way Is the Way

You may seek, receive, and experience, but not immediately get new thoughts or insights about how to proceed

>>

in your life. In this Online Extra I discuss how to handle the problem of experiencing from God, but still not seeing a way forward. This online extra is at

GatewaysToGod.com/way

How Sam Got His "R&R"

Let's get back to the example that started this chapter: Sam, the 55-year-old man who still found himself ogling college-age women. Let's look at how this process helped him go from remorse to return to being made new by God.

STEP 1: Ask yourself, "What is it costing me to act out this sin?" Sam felt guilty about his sin and knew he should stop looking at young women with lust. But as much as he disliked the fact that he was sinning, he hadn't taken the time to understand what that sinful behavior was costing him. So I asked him, "What is it costing you to act out this sin?"

"Well," he said, "I feel bad about it. These girls are so young and fresh and innocent, and when I look at them, I feel like I'm taking something from them. That's wrong."

"Okay," I said. "And when you feel like you are taking something from them, what is the cost to **you**?"

"I feel like I'm a 'dirty old man' and a 'taker,'" he said. "That's not who I want to be. Being a 'dirty old man' makes me feel ashamed, and taking from these young women makes me hate myself."

We now knew the cost to him of this sin. He felt like a "dirty old man," a "taker" who stole something from innocent young women. That was not who he wanted to be.

STEP 2: Feel your heartbreak about being stuck with the cost of your sin. "Now," I said, "you also have to feel your heartbreak about being stuck with the cost of your sin. How does it feel, in your heart, to be a 'dirty old man' who is taking something from innocent young women?"

"Ouch," he said. His face became ashen as he fully experienced the impact his behavior was having on his heart. "It hurts! It really hurts me to live that way." The cost was no longer just an idea to him. It was real and he felt it. And that reality gave him the motivation he needed to wholeheartedly move on to the next step.

STEP 3: Ask yourself, "What do I feel like I get out of this sinful behavior that I'd have a hard time doing without?" I knew Sam could easily say, "I want to change." But I also knew that what he'd really mean was, "I **should** want to change." He could "talk a good game" about changing, but that wasn't enough. Sam was so ashamed about his looking at women that he had a hard time admitting that it wasn't some weird behavior that just "happened to him." But his looking wasn't a random accident. He looked because he felt like he got something out of it that he needed. Before he could change, he had to be honest about that truth.

I told him, "We often can't give up sinful behaviors because we believe that those behaviors give us something we need. If you want to change your sinful behavior, you have to be honest about the part of you that feels like you are benefitting from it. So even though that behavior is a sin, I ask you: what does it seem like you are getting from looking at women that you feel like you might have a hard time doing without?"

The question made him stop and think. "At first I want to say 'nothing,'" he told me. "After all, looking at these young women with lust is a sin. But the truth is, there's a way in which it seems like it feeds me when I look at them. It gives me a charge, kind of like a cup of coffee. I do feel like it would be hard to do without the charge I get from looking at them. I do feel like I need those moments in order to make it through the day."

STEP 4: **Notice the impossible choice you are faced with.** "That's right," I said, "and you are courageous to admit it. Now notice the choice that it feels like you are stuck with: You can either sin, and get the charge that you feel like you need, or you can choose not to sin, but have to do without the charge that seems to help you make it through the day. Let yourself feel how hard it is to be in that position."

He sighed. "You're right. It does feel like an impossible choice. I try to stop looking, but my need for that charge finally gets the best of me, and I look again. It seems like I'm fated to have to sin and look or to starve inside by not looking. I feel stuck."

STEP 5: Go to God with the question, "Is this choice really true?" "Okay," I said. "We've explored the remorse, and we understand the impossible choice your sin seems to leave you with. Now it's time to return to God by going to Him with the question, 'Is this choice really true?' Do that," I added, "by **seeking** God with your neediness."

Sam had worked with me before, and he knew the process of seeking God. "Okay," he said. "Here I go. I am needy for You, O Lord, to know if I'm really stuck with either looking at women or doing without the energy I need. I am needy for You, O Lord, to know if that choice is true."

We sat together for several minutes as he **sought** and **received** from God. "I'm starting to feel like a beautiful light is shining on me," he finally said. "It's filling me up. I'm starting to feel as if all those dark places in me are becoming filled by light." His voice grew deeper and more relaxed. "I feel like I'm being gently stroked, and loved. Wow, I'm sitting up straighter. I'm breathing more deeply. Wow."

I let him sit with that for a while, then said, "As you feel that sensation in your body, see if it coalesces into an emotion, a feeling. What feeling might it be?"

"It feels gentle, like the release of forgiveness," Sam said. "I feel God's forgiveness of me, and His gentle love of me. That's different—before this, I was only feeling blame."

We sat in silence together as he **experienced** the gentle sensations of forgiveness and love. "So," I asked him at last, "from this point of view of gentle love and forgiveness, is this choice really the truth? Are you really stuck being a 'dirty old man' and taking from young women? Is that really what you have to do to get what you need?"

"No," he said firmly. "It's not. From this gentle feeling of forgiveness and love, I'm starting to see that I'm not meant to be someone who makes young women uncomfortable by looking at them with lust. I'm actually meant to be a source of safety for them. You know," he continued, "there once was a time when older men were a refuge for young women. Older men were the ones young women could go to in times of trouble. As I feel God's gentle love and forgiveness for me, I see that I am meant to be one of those men. I am meant to be an island of safety for young women. I'm meant to be a resource for them, a giver rather than a taker. Wow, that's really true—and it feels really different."

STEP 6: Notice how you are remade as a new creation. When you imagine yourself in the situation where you used to sin, what is different now? "From this new point of view," I asked, "what's different? Do you think it will be difficult to give up looking at young women with lust?"

"Absolutely not!" he said. "I'm meant to be a resource, a source of strength, of safety, of refuge. Being that source feels really, really good—much better than looking at them with lust ever felt. I actually feel charged up in a much better way. This is a big improvement. Thank you, God! I'll take it!"

Sam had **been made new**.

Living the Christian Life of Being Made New

Jesus tells his followers to "repent, for the kingdom of heaven is near" (Matthew 4:17). It worries me that many Christians hear this as a threat—that the kingdom of heaven is coming, so they'd better get their act together and repent already, or something bad is going to happen to them. It reminds me of a bumper sticker I once saw: "Jesus is coming—look busy!" As if the nearness of heaven is something we need to fear.

"Repent, for the kingdom of heaven is near" is a **promise**, not a threat. It's a promise that His kingdom is near, and that repentance is the entrance to it. I believe that when Jesus tells us to repent, he's inviting us to keep returning to God and to experience the kingdom of heaven for ourselves.

You can use this process on yourself any time you feel stuck in your sin and need some "R&R" so you can be made new.

The only remaining gateway for you to learn is how to **overflow with mercy** into every part of yourself— even to the parts of you for which you have "mercy exceptions."

Gateway Five:
Overflow with Mercy

"Oh yeah?" the man in front of me snarled. "Try **my** life!"

I was leading a group of fourteen surprisingly angry Christian men. Normally that wouldn't have bothered me, but they were all angry with **me,** which got my attention.

The other men in the group nodded in agreement with the man who was speaking. It was Friday evening, the beginning of our weekend together at a retreat center, and within ten minutes I'd made the whole group angry. I'd upset groups before, but this was the first time I'd done it so quickly.

I was surprised by their anger, because what I'd said to set them off seemed pretty basic to our faith. But I've noticed that when I do my work, I sometimes act as a catalyst for people to quickly bring forward hidden truths about their lives. That was happening here.

I had simply said that, at the end of the day, God is merciful, and that His mercy outweighs His wrath. And that simple statement had brought forth the anger I was now seeing.

I mean, "God is merciful" doesn't seem like a controversial claim, right? I said, "I seem to recall some verse in the Bible, let me see…something about God loving the world so much that He gave His only begotten Son? Something like that?" You may be thinking about that verse, too, perhaps along with other verses about the merciful nature of God, such as "O give thanks unto the Lord; for He is good: for His mercy endures forever" (Psalm 136:1), or "But because of His great love for us, God, who is rich in mercy, made us alive with Christ even when we were dead in transgressions—it is by grace you have been saved" (Ephesians 2:4-5).

But the problem these men had wasn't with those verses. Their problem was with the evidence of their lives, which left them feeling like God is **not** merciful. I could have spent the entire weekend quoting verses about God's mercy, and at the end of it they'd still have been a roomful of men who didn't believe God was merciful and who had spent the weekend being told they were wrong for feeling that way. That would not have been much help.

Quoting verses about God's mercy wasn't going to make a difference to these men because their hearts could not relate to the truth of those verses. God's mercy just wasn't on the menu for them. Telling them they were wrong to feel how they felt was certainly an option, but it wasn't going to make anything any better.

To make a long story short, by the end of our weekend together every man in that room agreed, in his heart, that God is merciful. But we had to do some work to get there, because each man in that room was suffering from a "mercy exception."

What Is a Mercy Exception?

You have a mercy exception when you believe that there is some part of you that is too terrible for God to love, and therefore is an exception to His mercy.

To be clear: You probably don't consciously think that any part of you is an exception to God's mercy. The men on my weekend didn't arrive consciously believing that some part of themselves was too terrible, even for God. But when I stood strongly in the conviction that God is merciful, all their hidden resistance to that idea surfaced. And it surfaced all at once.

These were men who could quote the Bible. They knew the verses about God's mercy as well as or better than I did. But over the course of the weekend, they each discovered that they were living as though a part of them was too terrible for God to love. Being with me on this weekend hadn't caused that belief. Being with me had merely brought that belief to light.

The Most Common Mercy Exceptions

While there is some variation in mercy exceptions from person to person, we can isolate two of major areas where Christians unconsciously decide that "this part of me is the exception to God's mercy."

Sexual fantasies. I encounter this problem mostly among Christian men, but also among some Christian women. I know of no area where Christian men withhold themselves from God's mercy more than they do around their sexual fantasies. This mercy exception does affect women, too—some Christian women I've known will have a mercy exception on themselves for having sexual dreams. For these men and women, the sins of their sexuality are exceptions to God's mercy.

Food and body issues. I encounter this problem mostly among Christian women, but also among some Christian men. I know of no area where Christian women withhold themselves from God's mercy more than they do around their behaviors with food, and the unhealthy, overweight bodies that result from the food they eat. For these women and men, their sins of overeating are exceptions to God's mercy.

Mercy exception sins are the ones that you just can't seem to handle, no matter how hard you try. No matter how much you ask for God to lift them from you, they don't seem to change. When you act them out you really harm yourself, or you really harm others. They are a big deal.

And while your mercy exception may be different, the odds are it's one of these: Something about your sexuality, or something about your body.

"There's Some Really Dark Stuff in Me that I Don't Know How to Handle."

As we proceeded through the weekend and men started sharing, exploring, and healing their mercy exceptions, they kept saying variations of, "There's some really dark stuff in me that I don't know how to handle."

In Christian circles, we are encouraged to confess to what are sometimes called "safe sins." Safe sin confessions are on the level of, "I was jealous of a co-worker's big promotion," or "I've been watching too much TV lately." We can confess these sins and receive some mercy about them precisely because they seem like the sort of sins that we ourselves could forgive. We can imagine ourselves as dignified, upstanding people who sometimes commit these sins. We can imagine forgiving others for them. Safe sins don't mess with our ability to think of ourselves as "good."

"Mercy exceptions" are different. They are the drives inside us — mostly around sex and food — that we really, really wish weren't there. In the face of those drives, we feel helpless and out of control. We experience intense but fleeting physical pleasure when we act them out, and a legitimate fear of what other Christians might think of us if they found out that we have them. And on top of all of that we experience an intense, overwhelming shame about having those drives at all.

When you believe there is a desire in you that is so terrible that it is an exception to God's mercy, you won't be likely to confess it. Instead you'll be likely to deny it. You'll hope it will go away, and try to hide it from other people and from God, until you somehow finally fix it yourself.

That's life with a mercy exception.

Core Christian Mercy Number Five

I love this Christian mercy:

> There's no part of you that
> is too terrible for God.

While the Bible is very clear that you are not condemned, and that you are loved even as Christ loved tax collectors, crooks, whores, and lepers, most Christians don't know how to experience God's love around their mercy exceptions.

Romans 8:1 tell us, "There is no condemnation for those who are in Jesus Christ." But how do you know for sure that you are "in Jesus Christ"? For many Christians, the mere fact that they have "unsafe sins" means they are **not** "in Jesus Christ." So they put off receiving that mercy until the imaginary day when they finally, on their own, get their mercy exception sins under control. But that day never comes.

Christian Roadblock Number Five

Christian Roadblock Number Five is:

> Christians try to get closer to God
> by having a "Mercy Exception."

Christians know that God's mercy outweighs His wrath, because "God so loved the world that He gave His one and only Son" for it. That's an act of ultimate mercy, not of ultimate wrath. The real God is the highest source of mercy that exists. But Christians who are trying to get closer to God by having mercy exceptions don't experience a merciful God. They can't even conceive of such a thing.

In fact,

> Christians in the grip of a mercy
> exception have stopped believing in
> a merciful God. They believe instead
> in a merciless idol.

Most Christians don't often think about the idea of believing in idols, because, hey—once you have accepted Christ's gift, you believe in the real God, right? You're saved, so you don't believe in any false "gods" anymore, right?

Surprisingly, the answer is often "no." You are saved, but even so, turning away from idols is not a "one-time" thing.

Sure, there are plenty of times in our lives when we believe in and experience the love of the highest, most merciful God. But because we can't imagine being forgiven for our mercy exceptions, there are other times when it is a lot easier for us to **turn to and believe in a merciless idol of our own invention,** which is just as unmerciful to us as we are to ourselves.

There's good news and bad news—and I'll tell you the bad news first. The bad news is that Christians are quite capable of switching back and forth from believing in the highest, most merciful God to a false, merciless idol very quickly. We can make that switch many times a day. And we usually don't even notice when we are switching.

But there's good news, too: Once you understand that you sometimes believe in a merciless idol, you can return to the merciful God, even from the depths of a mercy exception. Isaiah 55:7 says, "Let the wicked forsake his way, and the unrighteous man his thoughts: and let him return unto the Lord, and He will have mercy upon him; and to our God, for He will abundantly pardon." You can return to God's abundant pardon, and experience it, even though there are parts of you that you sometimes think are exceptions to God's mercy. That is good news.

God says, "You shall have no other gods before Me" (Exodus 20:3), so this is important: If you're going to live in God's grace—not just as an idea, but as a real, living experience, every day of your life—then you **must** be able to identify when you have put an idol before Him. You must be able to identify that idol, and you must be able to turn from it, back to the mercy of God. The Christian roadblock is that we don't make that turn back to God. Instead we dwell in the realm of the merciless idol.

Is Your God Merciful?

We know that God is merciful. That doesn't mean that God is "nice," or that He will give you what you want when you want it, or that His guidance will be what your flesh wants to hear, or that His mercy is some sort of "diplomatic immunity" that allows you to continue in your sinful behaviors without any consequences. Just because He is merciful doesn't mean, "Hey, everything's cool, just keep on sinning." Sometimes God's mercy can seem pretty merciless, and the fact is that sin will lead to suffering—that is the order of things.

But God is merciful toward you even when you are at your worst. In fact, He says "I will never leave you nor forsake you" (Hebrews 13:5). You may feel forsaken, but God says that, even when you feel forsaken, He has never left you.

So God is merciful and God will never forsake you. Therefore, if you are believing in a god who is **not** merciful and who **has** forsaken you, the Bible itself says you are not believing in the real God.

You may be believing in something—you may be praying to something, you may be worshipping something, and you may be suffering under the judgment of something—but if that something is not merciful, and if that something has forsaken you, then that something is not God.

That "something" is a merciless idol.

Christian Challenge Number Five

In the face of our mercy exceptions, the fifth Christian Challenge is:

> To see the merciless idol for what it is,
> and to turn back to the true God.

Turning to God should connect you with His mercy for your heart. Again, that doesn't necessarily mean you'll be told what you want to hear or that you'll be "let off the hook" for bad behaviors. But turning to God should lead to mercy. If turning connects you with mercilessness instead, you are probably believing in an idol.

Sinning is absolutely a problem. But that problem is magnified, amplified, and "locked in" when you believe in a merciless idol. Believing in a merciless idol hardens the idea that there is no way forward, and that you really are beyond redemption—until you somehow fix yourself.

Having to fix your mercy exception sin by yourself is difficult because mercy exception sins (like all sins, really) can only be healed with God's help. But when you believe in a merciless idol, you're on your own. There is no help. Without God and facing a merciless idol, it's actually easier to continue the sinful behavior—the pornography, the binge eating, the whatever—than it is to risk being annihilated by such an unmerciful figure.

A person trying to heal his or her darkest desires and behaviors by turning to a merciless idol is like a person trying to get out of a hole by digging it even deeper. More mercilessness will never heal the part of you that needs mercy in order to change. It's never going to work. You have to see the merciless idol for what it is, and turn back to God.

And to do that, you need to **overflow with mercy.**

Christian Gateway Number Five: Overflow with Mercy

In the first gateway you learned to open your **seeking**. In the second gateway you discovered how to **receive** what you sought for. In the third gateway you learned to **experience** what you sought for and received, and in the fourth gateway you learned to **be made new** by that experience.

This fifth gateway—**overflowing with mercy**—is about extending the fourth gateway (being made new) to every single part of yourself—including the very worst parts of yourself. Overflowing with mercy means receiving God's mercy for every part of yourself, with no exceptions whatsoever. It means experiencing love, mercy, grace and healing, not just for your "safe sins," but for the parts of yourself that you secretly believe are beyond any hope of redemption. It means experiencing God's mercy not just a little, but so much so that it fills you up and overflows into every part of your being.

Overflowing with Mercy Is Hard

It's a tall order to live a life overflowing with mercy. You can't just focus your willpower to "mercy harder" or scold yourself into treating yourself more mercifully. Our nature is to be severe with ourselves, especially around our mercy exceptions. Overflowing with mercy doesn't come naturally to us and won't just happen on its own. If you're going to overflow with mercy, you're going to need God's help.

Opening the Gateway of Overflowing With Mercy

You overflow with mercy by seeing the merciless idol for what it is, and consciously turning back to God. You turn away from the unloving and return to the love. You stop receiving from a power that despises you and receive again from the loving God. I call this process "Idol Breaking."

Let me give you a couple of examples of Idol Breaking:

I had a client—I'll call him Alvin—who had trouble with pornography. He would look at it for hours. He became more upset and more miserable as each viewing incident went on, but he was unable to stop himself.

During his session, I asked him, "How do you feel when you finally stop looking?" "Terrible," he said. "I just try to go to sleep, or get busy with something, and try not to think about what I've done. It's just too horrible."

"You know," I said, "a lot of counselors would try to come up with ways to help you control this behavior.

They'd help you learn ways to have more willpower. Or they'd help you set up a series of blocks and blinders—like turning off your Internet access, or making sure you were never alone—to keep you from looking at pornography. Is that the kind of help you've gotten?"

"Yes," he said. "That's exactly how people have tried to help me. And all their ideas are really good, but it just seems like when I'm in that state of mind I can get past any blocker. My lust finds a way. I feel like I literally lose all control of myself."

"So," I said, "instead of trying to set up better structures to stop you from looking at pornography—which you'd overcome anyway—I first want to know more about the 'god' you are believing in when you are in the middle of a pornography session."

This was a new idea for him. "I guess I haven't thought about that," he said.

"I know," I said. "As a Christian, you know that if you are with God, you are forgiven for your behaviors, and if you repent, you are made new. But it's hard to experience being with God if what you are believing in is not actually God. Therefore we have to find out about the god you find yourself believing in, to make sure you actually are turning toward the real God."

I continued, "I want you to really experience what you are believing in. Imagine that you are in the midst of looking at pornography. Now this might seem a little strange, but I want you to tell me your best sense of what the god you are believing in might say about you while you are doing that."

"Wait. I'm supposed to say what I feel like the god I'm believing in says about me when I'm looking at porn?" he asked incredulously.

"Yes, that's exactly right."

Alvin took a deep breath and closed his eyes. "Okay," he said. He paused a moment and considered. "It feels to me like that god would say, 'I hate this man. I completely despise him. I'm disgusted with him and furious at him. I've given him so much, and this is what he chooses to do with it! I hate him and want to punish him for what he's doing, for how he's sinning against me and sinning against his body. I don't have the slightest bit of mercy for him. He's garbage, he's weak, and I hate him.'" His voice had grown louder and louder as he imagined this "god" berating him.

"Okay," I said. "That's pretty strong, but not unexpected. Now shift back into your own point of view again. Let me recap: When you are looking at pornography you are believing in a god who despises you, is disgusted by you, thinks you're garbage, doesn't have the slightest bit of mercy for you, and wants to punish you. That's what's going on, right?"

"Oh my goodness," he said, opening his eyes. "that's exactly what's going on! When I'm looking at porn, that's exactly the god I'm believing in."

"So when you turn to that god for help," I asked, "how does it work?"

"It doesn't work at all! That 'god' doesn't have any help for me — he hates me! When I turn to that hatred, I end up feeling more ashamed and alone, and more needy of something to make me feel better. It actually makes me look at more porn, and for longer — I know that the second I stop I'm going to have to contend with that hatred and disgust."

"So here's the big question," I said. "Is that being you are believing in, who has that hatred and disgust for you, really the highest, most merciful God that your heart can conceive of relating to?"

"Absolutely not," he said immediately. "I know God loves me, even though I am a sinner. But I'm believing in something that totally hates me, that wants to destroy me, that has no mercy for me. That's not God at all! If anything, it's more like the devil!"

He had identified his merciless idol. "Do you want to keep worshipping that?" I asked.

"No!"

"Then now is the time to turn away from that, to reject that merciless idol and to begin to seek God."

Alvin closed his eyes again. He leaned back and breathed deeply.

"When you reject this idol that hates you," I said, "and bring your sinning self to God's mercy, what do you experience?"

We sat together in silence as he sought God. "Ahhh," he said at last. "There really is mercy for me! There really is! It's like a huge sense of relief is flooding into my chest and into my heart. I can breathe more easily, more openly. God really does love me. He really does have forgiveness for me." We sat a while longer as he took his time experiencing the truth of that realization.

"I'm meant to be big with God," he eventually continued. "I'm meant to be so filled up by Him that His love flows out of me everywhere, all the time. I'm meant to be so connected to Him and to other people that I don't need anything more than that to be happy." His eyes teared up. "That feels so good. Oh, thank you, God. Thank you."

"Feel how this is changing you," I said. "Feel the man you are being made into. Does this man need to look at pornography?"

We sat in silence again while he sensed God's love for him as he pondered the answer to that question. "No," he said finally. "There is so much love for me to share with God and other people. I don't need porn to feel good."

"And if you do happen to backslide," I said, "even though you don't want to, what do you feel God would say to you?"

"I feel that God would say, 'I love you. That's why I want you not to sin.' He'd say, 'Feel My love, feel the love of the people who love you. Delight in that. Explode in the light of that! I invite you. I love you. I want you not to sin because I love you.' Wow! If I did get tempted, that sure would bring me back. That's a much better reason not to look at porn than 'because I shouldn't.' I want to have this closeness to God's love far more than I ever wanted to look at porn."

Alvin had been touched by God's mercy—and every time we are touched by His mercy, we are changed. Would that change be permanent? Quite possibly. This one experience may have been enough to transform his relationship with pornography forever.

But sometimes more than one experience of mercy and of change is necessary before a person is fully transformed. Alvin might need more experiences of God's mercy to become completely free of pornography. What's certain, however, is that after this experience he was well on his way to completing that transformation—because he had left behind the dark world of the mercy exception, and entered the realm of the mercy of God.

Overeating and the Mercy Exception

Another client, whom I'll call Hazel, told me about how she would lose control and overeat unhealthy foods. "I've tried every diet in the world," she said, "but I just don't have the willpower to say no to the sweet stuff. I'm just so weak! It tempts me and I just can't say no."

Hazel was seventy-five pounds overweight and had tried—really tried—to stop overeating. She'd made promises to stop her overeating. She'd tried support groups to stop her overeating. She'd tried increasingly complicated plans to ensure that she wouldn't be exposed to the foods that tempted her. She had instituted strict rules about what foods could and could not be brought into her house. And she had scolded herself again and again about her overeating. But none of these actions ever seemed to help her for long. She always ended up back in her pattern of losing control with food.

I told her, "Rather than focus on your overeating, I want you to focus on the 'god' you are believing in when you are engaged in overeating. Imagine that you are in the middle of overeating something—a box of cookies, perhaps. Now this might seem a little odd, but I want you to give me your best sense of what the god you are believing in might say about you while you are overeating."

Hazel leapt to the task. "I just ate a big box of cookies yesterday," she said, "so this is easy. That god is so disgusted with me. It's like he's saying, 'She's such a fat pig! I hate her. She's so disgusting and she keeps eating and eating and she's fat! I hate her so much!'"

"So does that god have mercy for Hazel?" I asked.

"Absolutely no mercy!" Hazel said. "That god thinks Hazel should just die!"

"Wow," I said. "That's some strong stuff. Now shift back into your own point of view. Let me recap: when you are in the midst of overeating, you are believing in a god who is disgusted with you, who hates you, who has no mercy for you, and wants you to die. Is that correct?"

"That's right," she admitted, "though I've never thought about it this way before. When I'm pigging out on cookies or whatever, I don't really think about the kind of god I'm believing in. But I can tell you that I **feel** it. I feel that hatred, that disgust, that doom hanging over my head."

"And how does it work," I asked, "when you reach out to that disgusted, hateful, merciless being for help when you are overeating?"

"Ha!" She laughed bitterly. "When I go to that being for help, I just get beaten up more! It's so angry with me, it only makes things worse. And then I feel so terrible that I really do need a cookie—and I might as well eat as many as I want, since I'm doomed either way."

"That's a good observation," I said. "So here's the big question: Is that being you are believing in the highest, most merciful God that your heart can conceive of relating to?"

"No," she said flatly. "No, no, no. God doesn't hate me. God loves me. God loves me a lot. He has mercy for me, not disgust. What I'm believing in totally hates me, so it can't be God."

She had identified her merciless idol and was seeing it for what it was. "Do you want to keep worshipping that?" I asked her.

"No! Absolutely not."

"Then now is the time to reject that merciless idol, to turn away from it, and to start seeking the real God."

Hazel closed her eyes and sat with the experience of turning away from her merciless idol. She began **seeking** the mercy she knew the real God had for her, then began **receiving** and **experiencing**. "I feel His warmth all over my body," she said at last. "The real God loves me—He doesn't hate me. He cares for me, no matter what. If I'm going through a difficult time, the real God is there with me. I can feel that, now."

We sat in silence together for several minutes more as Hazel felt God **making her new**. Finally I asked, "And as you feel His love, what new truths do you discover?"

"Well," Hazel replied, "when I'm in His love, I can feel that there's a purpose for me. There's a path for my life. And, difficult as that sometimes is, I'm on that path. And on that path He's making me into something." We sat together as she absorbed this new insight. Finally I asked, "From this love that you are feeling, what does it feel like He's making you into?"

"He's making me into someone who is light, both in my heart and in my body." Her face lit up as she spoke. "I can feel it. I actually feel lighter, like a weight has been lifted from me. My shoulders feel lighter. I feel lifted up. I feel like He's feeding me what I really need, but I feel lighter!" She paused. "This is the manna. This is the food of God."

"Does this woman you are being made into need to overeat?" I asked.

"No," she said. "I am fed. My heart is fed by God. From the knowledge that God is feeding me, I feel like I could actually turn my back on a box of cookies. God's love is the cookie I've always wanted."

"And if you do happen to backslide," I asked, "even though you don't want to, how do you feel that God would respond to you?"

"I feel like God would look at me with love, not with anger or hatred. He would reach a hand out to me with the manna I need. He would always welcome me back."

Living the Christian Life of Overflowing with Mercy

Mercy exceptions are very personal. We don't like sharing them with others. But you can take a few moments now to share your mercy exceptions with God.

FIRST, IDENTIFY YOUR MERCY EXCEPTION. Many Christians are not aware they have a mercy exception until they look for it. Ask yourself what sin of yours seems too terrible for God — so much so that you feel as if you have to get rid of it before you can receive God's mercy. It may be something about sex, it may be something about food, or it may be something else entirely, but you'll know it because it will seem irredeemable. That's your mercy exception.

SECOND, FIND YOUR MERCILESS IDOL. After you've identified your mercy exception, ask yourself, "When I am acting out that behavior, what's my best sense of what God thinks of me?" Be honest and answer from your gut. Don't just ask your smart brain for the "right" answer (which will be, "Of course He loves me!"). Instead, speak from what you are actually experiencing, rather than from what you "ought to" experience.

If you experience mercy from God, that's great — let yourself soak it up. But if your best sense of what God thinks of you is merciless, then you've found your merciless idol — and it's time to see that for what it really is, reject it, and to turn back to the real God.

THIRD, REJECT THE MERCILESS IDOL AND SEEK THE MERCY OF THE REAL GOD. You have to be willing to say, "I may not know what God really has for me, but since what I'm believing in isn't merciful, I know it's not that." You then **seek** with your heart, to **receive**, to

experience, and to **be made new** by the real highest, most merciful God.

Again: "merciful" isn't necessarily the same as "nice" or "telling you what you want to hear." But even if you are feeling challenged by what you sense God has for you, you should still be able to connect to His mercy for your heart. If there's no mercy for you until you somehow change yourself though your own will and your own effort, then you are probably still believing in a merciless idol.

FINALLY, EXPERIENCE HOW YOU ARE CHANGED BY WHAT YOU RECEIVE. As you live with this new mercy, how might you naturally behave differently going forward? How might God be there for you if you should backslide, even though you don't want to? Let yourself experience the answer to those questions as you imagine what your life might be like as you move forward with God's mercy.

Discovering God's Mercy for Yourself

Christians in the grip of a mercy exception make the mistake of believing in—and trying to receive help from—a "god" who is as merciless about their sins as they themselves are. But Jonah 2:8 tells us that "those who cling to worthless idols turn away from God's love for them." It doesn't matter how many times you go to a merciless idol: doing so will **never** bring love, relief, or healing to your heart. When you are believing in a merciless idol, any changes you make to your behavior won't last, because they will be wholly dependent on your own willpower. If you want to be healed of your mercy exception sin, **you must break the grip of the merciless idol and return to the real mercy of God.**

Alvin and Hazel had broken the grip of their merciless idol and returned to the love of God. During our weekend together, the men I spoke of at the start of this chapter each had a similar experience. Each man found his merciless idol, rejected it, and returned his heart to the mercy of God.

We each have to discover God's mercy for ourselves. That's part of the challenge and the delight of being Christian. But we'll never succeed if we are trying to receive that mercy from anything less than the highest, most merciful God.

The Five Gateways and Living a Life of Closeness with God

Throughout this book I've emphasized that participating emotionally in your life is an essential part of living in closeness with God. When you pass through a Gateway to God, you use the circumstances of your life, along with all your reactions to those circumstances, as your means for drawing closer to Him.

Let's review the gateways I've shared in this book:

1. DRAWING CLOSER TO GOD THROUGH THE GATEWAY OF SEEKING. Drawing closer to God through the gateway of seeking means knowing your need for God like a drowning person knows his or her need for air.

The good news is that when you authentically know your need for God, your heart will start to **seek** for Him with urgency and persistence. You'll seek God "with all your heart and all your soul" (Deuteronomy 4:29).

2. DRAWING CLOSER TO GOD THROUGH THE GATEWAY OF RECEIVING. Drawing closer to God through the gateway of receiving means feeling how your efforts to "balance the books" with God have left you weary and burdened.

The good news is that when you honestly lay down your burdened weariness before God, your heart will start to **receive** the love He has for you. You'll discover the truth that "my yoke is easy and my burden is light" (Matthew 11:30).

3. DRAWING CLOSER TO GOD THROUGH THE GATEWAY OF EXPERIENCING. Drawing closer to God through the gateway of experiencing means feeling the ways in which living to fulfill the Christian Checklist has kept you from the flowing, alive nature of God.

The good news is that when you authentically acknowledge how striving to fulfill a checklist makes the living, flowing God into a static to-do list, your heart will begin to go beyond that checklist to **experience** what God has for you through your body, your emotions, and your insights. You'll taste the truth that "Whoever drinks the water I give them will never thirst. Indeed, the water I give them will become in them a spring of water welling up to eternal life" (John 4:14).

4. DRAWING CLOSER TO GOD THROUGH THE GATEWAY OF BEING MADE NEW. Drawing closer to God by being made new means acknowledging how heartbroken you become when you fall into the trap of believing that your sinful behavior is the only way to get something that you need.

The good news is that when you genuinely experience that heartbreak, your heart will begin to return to God to **be made new**. You will live the truth of "I will give you a new heart and put a new spirit in you; I will remove from you your heart of stone and give you a heart of flesh" (Ezekiel 36:26).

5. DRAWING CLOSER TO GOD THROUGH THE GATEWAY OF OVERFLOWING WITH MERCY. Drawing closer to God by overflowing with mercy means acknowledging the sinful parts of you that you believe are too terrible for God to love, then rejecting the merciless idol that you have turned toward and returning to the merciful love of God.

The good news is that when you reject the merciless idols you've been facing, **overflowing with mercy** can transform your deepest sins. You'll be able to join other Christians as we cry out, "Let us then approach God's throne of grace with confidence, so that we may receive mercy and find grace to help us in our time of need" (Hebrews 4:16).

Now that you know about these gateways, it's time to start looking at the problems, circumstances, and emotions of your life and to ask yourself: "Which gateway do I need to pass through in order to experience God's love and mercy for me in this situation?"

- Do you need to seek, by stating your need to God?

- Do you need to receive, by laying down your burden before Him?

- Do you need to experience what He has for you, through your body, your emotions, and your insights?

- Do you need to be made new, by confessing to Him the sinful behavior you feel you can't do without?

- Do you need to overflow with mercy, by rejecting a merciless idol and returning to His mercy and His love?

If you don't know where to start, simply start at the beginning: you'll never go wrong by seeking God. Then pass through the other gateways as you feel ready, one gateway at a time.

Online Extra: Making the Gateways Part of Your Life

If you're going to live a life of experiencing closeness with God, you're going to need ongoing support. Remember, Christ said, "When two or three come together in my name, there I am with them" (Matthew 18:20). Christ encourages us to not "go it alone."

>>

While reading these pages may be useful to you, if you want to have more than just the experience of reading a book—if you want to truly integrate these ideas into your moment-to-moment experience of life—then you'll need to "come together" with others who also want to use these tools to draw closer to God.

You may wish to share this book with others at your church and to discuss and practice the exercises with them (contact me for study guides and group facilitation materials).

You may also wish to join the free online community that goes along with this book, at GatewaysToGod.com. I regularly post articles and short videos that answer questions and give bite-sized, easy-to-use tips and ideas for living in the experience of God's love. I also run workshops and tele-classes, and offer a limited number of individual phone sessions.

I hope you'll decide to join us, and that at some point you and I can get to know each other personally.

GatewaysToGod.com/blog

You can also follow me on twitter @DmitriBilgere, and connect with me by "liking" me on Facebook at Facebook.com/DmitriBilgere.

The Kingdom of God Begins in Your Heart

Imagine a rock tossed into a still pond. After the initial splash, ripples from the impact radiate in widening circles in all directions across the water.

That tossed rock is like God's love and mercy for you. When His love splashes into the pond of your heart—when you **seek** His love and mercy, **receive** it, **experience** it, are **made new** by it, and let your heart **overflow** with it—it creates ripples of love, mercy, and virtuous behavior that radiate effortlessly outward from you.

Those ripples of love first touch every part of you, then they move outwards and touch the members of your family, and the people you encounter in your work and in your community. Ultimately, that love, and the behaviors that flow effortlessly from it, touch the entire world.

I don't believe that we build God's kingdom on Earth by trying to change external situations or other people before we are changed ourselves. I believe we build His kingdom on Earth by setting our hearts to the task of becoming overflowing rivers of His love and His mercy. But we can't overflow with that love if we don't first have it, abundantly, in our hearts for ourselves.

When we Christians live as abundant, overflowing rivers of His love, our actions will naturally bring love, mercy, justice, peace and freedom to the world. Together, that's how we build God's kingdom on Earth.

Acknowledgments

Writing this book has been a process of revelation. I consistently felt as if I wasn't so much creating something, as I was uncovering something that was already there and patiently waiting for me to reveal it. Any success I've had in doing so is entirely due to the blessings of God, and any failure is entirely my own. I have nothing but gratitude for the gifts He has given me in this process.

Once such gift is the people who helped me with the inspiration, writing and production of this book. Most of all I have to thank my wife, Fawn, whose steadfast support kept me going when I felt like giving up. More than any other person, it is because of her that you have this book to read.

I also wish to thank these people for their invaluable help (listed in alphabetical order):

Kyle Arney
Bert Botta
Carol Brown
Amanda Bryson
Roger Cameron

Lyman Coleman
Richard Ely
Rob Ely
Kevin Evanko
Brian E.

Jack Gallaway
Jay Goldstein
Katherine Harms
Aaron Harsch
Doug Harsch
Daphne Meyers
Jan Hook
Kristyn Kalnes

James Keeley
Dave Long
Doug McBride
Nicole Sundquist
John Tittle
Sans Talbot
Paul Schlegel
Shawn Swinigan

I know that once this book goes to press I'm sure to think of some people I forgot to thank. If you are one of them, please know I am grateful for your help.